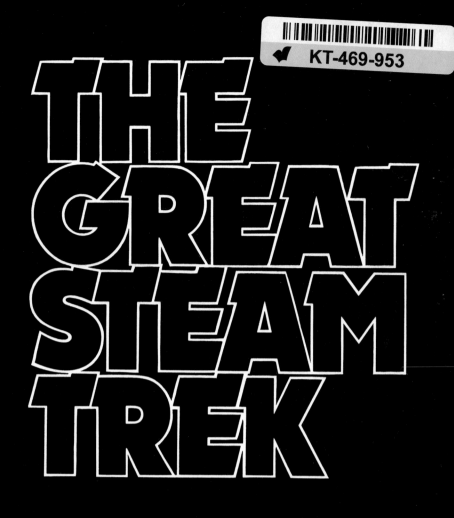

THE GREAT STEAM TREK

C.P. LEWIS
A.A. JORGENSEN

THE GREAT STEAM TREK

HAMLYN
LONDON · NEW YORK · SYDNEY · TORONTO

Contents

This edition published by
The Hamlyn Publishing Group Limited,
London · New York · Sydney · Toronto
Astronaut House, Feltham, Middlesex, England
Copyright © A.A. Jorgensen and C.P. Lewis 1978

ISBN 0 600 38315 6

Introduction

The Trans-Karoo Express, her 4-8-4 freshly watered at Orange River, moves purposefully up the grade to Witput, showers of cinders striking steel coach roofs. On the footplate are the regular crew and, learning the road, an old driver just transferred from Pietermaritzburg. He is accustomed to 1 in 30 grades on 5-chain reverse curves and has never been so fast on an engine in his life, but he's enjoying the bucking and swaying in a nervous sort of way. The gradient steepens to 1 in 100, the drag of 17 steel coaches matching the 3 000 hp of the engine as she settles down to a steady 40 mph. The grinding of the stoker worm working hard can be heard above the roar of the engine, cutting off at 45% with regulator wide open.

Suddenly a violent acceleration of the stoker motor indicates a snapped worm, and coal delivery ceases, causing consternation in the cab. When this happens, a crew would not normally be blamed for throwing in the sweat rag and calling for a replacement engine: 70 square feet of grate takes a lot of keeping hot. But the old driver from Maritzburg is no ordinary soul. He despatches the fireman to the tender to trim coal towards the shovel-plate, picks up the scoop and rhythmically hand-feeds the huge firebox. He never hurries, but makes each scoopful count. Nor does he stop shovelling, for by the time he has done one round of the grate it is time to start on the next. For over an hour he is on his feet, feeding the firebox and making it look easy. The train draws into Kimberley on time, her sleeping passengers unaware of the exertions of the three men up front. But the figures tell the story: 800 tons of train have been brought 70 miles, mostly uphill, in 90 minutes, and in that time over 5 000 lbs of coal have been manhandled into the firebox.

Countless such stories could be told of the daily feats of steam men and their trains, for they are a unique breed. Year in and year out they spend up to 100 hours a week on the footplate, and yet find time to polish and care for their engines.

Much has been written about the early 19th century Voortrekkers and their achievements, but the Great Steam Trek is as important in the history of South Africa as the Great Trek by oxwagon. When one considers that 100 years ago steam trains were hauling 200 tons of goods at 20 mph (as compared with two tons at two mph for an oxwagon); that the first railway electrification was not until the twenties; and that the first effective national road network was only started in the thirties, it becomes clear that while it was the Voortrekkers who opened up South Africa, it was the steam locomotive which enabled the country to be developed.

This book is a pictorial tribute to the unsung heroes of the Great Steam Trek – the men who keep the trains rolling, and their locomotives.

Preface

The golden age of steam on South African railways lasted a long time. It may be said to have begun in the 1890s with the arrival of the first engines designed locally for local conditions; and it continued until the early 1950s when the last new classes arrived. The zenith was reached towards the close of the Hendrie era, in the mid-20s, when our railways were still 100% steam-operated. Thereafter a decline set in as electrification and then dieselization became ever more widespread; but the decline here was slower than in other countries, primarily because of the fuel position in South Africa. Except for the output of the oil-from-coal plant at Sasolburg, all oil must be imported, whereas there is an abundance of indigenous coal, and this is why even today steam has a significant, though diminishing, role to play in transportation on the subcontinent.

THE GREAT STEAM TREK is not intended to be a comprehensive account of this golden age, but is an attempt to capture the essence of steam railways in South Africa as we have known them. Because the steam locomotive is slowly dying out, even in this country, our approach has been nostalgic and pictorial with a text consisting of historical background and anecdotes to supplement the photographs and their captions. We have chosen the pictures carefully: quality has only been sacrificed for rarity. If they convey the fascination of a railway operated by steam, then we shall have achieved our objective.

The quality and variety of these photographs is in no small measure due to the countless railwaymen who patiently answered questions about the running of trains, or coaxed ancient machines out onto the road. We especially thank Messrs P. L. Aucamp, Willie Deysel, Frans Geldenhuys, Pat Lovell, Steve Verster, Frans Victor and Alec Watson for their enthusiastic support. The help of the many engine crews who provided a bit of smoke at just the right moment is greatly appreciated.

While on the subject of smoke: to many of us the exhaust from a steam locomotive is aesthetically appealing, particularly as it is a visual manifestation of its power; but many pollution-conscious laymen will look in horror at the almost volcanic eruptions shown in these pages. We ask them to bear in mind that these clouds consist mostly of harmless steam and particulate matter and are not nearly as toxic as the lead-laden fumes coughed into the atmosphere by the thousands of cars in our cities.

Our sincere thanks are due to the many photographers (credited on page 246) who have allowed us to use some of their finest work.

We are also indebted to Mr Eric Conradie of the SAR Library, and to Messrs Frank G. Garrison and Helmuth Hagen, both professional railwaymen, who provided invaluable information and advice on the text.

C. P. Lewis   A. A. Jorgensen 1978

1 At an estimated 70 mph, 'A. G. Watson' heads the special northbound Union Express on 17 September 1977. Named after her designer, Class 16E Pacific No. 858 is one of a class of six built by Henschel of Germany in 1935. With 72″ driving wheels, a 21-ton axle-load and 40 000-lb tractive effort, they were easily the largest narrow-gauge passenger locomotives ever built, bigger than many European Pacifics on the standard gauge.

2 On a cold overcast Karoo morning in July 1976, 25NC 4-8-4 No. 3452 emerges from its own steam cover as it advances upgrade, south from Orange River. It is one of a class of 90 which formerly operated as condensing engines. From 1973 on when these engines went through shops the condensing gear was removed, and they thus became free-exhausting for the first time after nearly twenty years of operation. At the beginning of 1978 only about 30 engines remained unconverted, and these are expected to be converted during the next two years – all but one, which will go to the Railway Museum.

3 *Narrow, narrow gauge.* By American and European standards, South Africa's railways are all narrow-gauge, the width between the rails being 3′ 6″ instead of 4′ 8½″. But there are several hundred miles of even narrower lines with only 2′ between the rails. One of these, the Port Elizabeth-Avontuur line, is well known to tourists because a special train, the 'Apple Express', runs during the summer season and is very well patronised. But it is also a working railway with proper trains for general cargo. This scene is at Loerie, at the foot of a steep grade. In the early morning sun Garratt locomotives prepare for a day's work.

4 A GEA has its fire cleaned at Bot River.

5 A little spit and polish.

6 Approaching Pretoria with a 15CA on a Saturdays-only train from Cullinan to Pretoria.

7 Trailing bissel oil cup, 12AR.

8 The grease-stained motion of 25NC No. 3449.

9 A 15CA at Bronkhorstspruit.

10 Dousing the ashes.

11 No. 2069, one of the beautifully groomed 15CBs, once kept by Krugersdorp shed.

12 Fetching the fire irons.

13 Early morning activities on the ash pits at Bloemfontein, May 1977.

14 In the cold light of a Transvaal winter dawn, a steam train breaks the stillness as it charges along the rails of Witbank Colliery. The Witbank area is the centre of one of the largest coal deposits in the Southern Hemisphere and some two dozen collieries operate here. Many of these maintain lengthy railway lines – and most remain faithful to the locomotive that burns the fuel they mine.

15 Here, in her prime, is the unique No. 781 on the 5.36 pm Cape Town-Strand in April 1956. After being rebuilt from Beatty's enlarged Karoo-type to A. G. Watson's specifications with standard boiler, piston valves and 5′ 2″ wheels, she became the only Class 5R and a redoubtable performer. With her Stephenson link motion and long-travel valves she went like a cannonball with a rifle-shot exhaust. For nearly 20 years she was allocated to driver Best, who had her tuned to perfection. Some years after she had been condemned for scrapping in 1967, an alert RSSA (Railway Society of Southern Africa) member, Tony Elliott, spotted her rusting away on a back road at the Salt River workshops, and she was fortunately rescued for preservation.

16 Belpaire 6C No. 553 takes the 3.43 pm Malmesbury semi-fast out of Cape Town in September 1955. For many years this train was entrusted to the various types of Class 6, and occasionally to the 5Bs.

1 The Cape Main Line

Up country

For those of us fortunate enough to have been born in the Cape, anywhere beyond the confines of the Cape Peninsula was 'in the country', and anywhere beyond the first blue range of mountains guarding the interior was 'up country'. Gabriel Bayman

The Cape Main Line has always been South Africa's most romantic railway. Diamond diggers seeking their fortunes in the mines at Kimberley, *uitlanders* rushing to the fabulous gold deposits on the Witwatersrand, the Ridge of White Waters, troops bound for the Anglo-Boer War, opportunists, immigrants, goods and materials for Rhodes's Cape-to-Cairo railway have all used this route, imbuing it with a history unsurpassed on the South African Railways. And it is on the Cape Main Line that the top trains and most glamorous motive power have run. For 94 years steel wheels driven by expanding steam rolled out of Cape Town for 'up country'. It was not an easy road. The long grades and high passes set standards for some of the most powerful locomotives ever to run on narrow-gauge rails.

The early engines were ordered overseas to specifications prepared locally by Michael Stephens, first Locomotive Superintendent of the Cape Government Railways (CGR). But the first really effective ones were designed in the CGR's workshops at Salt River by H. M. Beatty, whose 4-8-0 (of 1892) would become SAR Class 7 and his 4-6-0 (of 1893) SAR Class 6. These venerable machines survived in large numbers into the sixties. From 1902, the 6s and 7s were joined by another very successful Beatty design, the Class 8. These three classes virtually monopolised operations – with increasing assistance in later years from Classes 4, 5 and 4A (Beatty) and 10C (Elliot) – until the arrival of D. A. Hendrie's masterpiece, the 15A. From 1915 until the thirties the 15A ruled the heavy rail, although edged out of the top jobs after 1925 by 'Big Bill' and his brother 15CBs.

The 15CBs and the later 15CAs altered the course of South African locomotive history as radically as Hendrie's magnificent designs had done a decade earlier. Gone were the plate frames, conservative boiler heights and low running-plates favoured by Hendrie. Now the American school took over – and many would say that this was no improvement, in looks at least.

From 1925 and on through the depression years the premier trains were entrusted to the American engines, but by 1935 the influence of another inspired Chief Mechanical Engineer, A. G. Watson, was manifesting itself in the shape of the 'Bongol', the heavy poppet-valved 4-8-2 of Class 15E. The nickname came from the Zulu word for donkey, but it is not known whether it applied to the 15E's propensity for work, or to the labours of the fireman who had to keep its 63 square feet of grate hot!

The Bongols were partially replaced over the Cape Town-Beaufort West section by W. A. J. Day's Class 23 of 1937. From 1943 onwards the Class 15F, a mechanically-fired, Walschaert-motioned version of the Bongol, played an increasing rôle, and the 15Es were moved to the relatively fast Beaufort West-De Aar section. It was along here in 1953 that we timed a 15E for 11 consecutive miles at over 70 mph on a 15-coach relief Orange Express. When running at high speed, the Bongols had a rapid, square-clipped exhaust, akin to the purr of an internal combustion machine.

When the electrification from Cape Town to Touws River was completed, Paarden Eiland shed had a fleet of 48 15Fs and six 23s for the main line. That was in 1954, and the railway would never be the same again. It took another three years for the traditions of over 90 years to die, but by 1957 the inevitable had happened and the last of the 15Fs had been drafted away. The last batch went to Port Elizabeth where they would see another 12 years of top link service.

17 *Bound for the city of gold.* A majestic Hendrie Class 15A No. 1802 threads her way towards the high rails with the Union Express in February 1928. The Buren wing of the Castle on the left stood sentinel for decades over the old station, where main-line trains left for 'up country'. Busy as an ocean liner's quayside at sailing time, platforms 12, 13 and (later) 14 were the only ones where you needed a platform ticket merely to wave goodbye. Having bought one from a tickey slot-machine, you were admitted to the mêlée of well-wishers, passengers, baggage and porters crying 'Maaind the berro!' Above the hubbub you could hear the sing-song call of the postal workers loading mail bags for faraway places like Pot-gieters-rus, Hope-town and War-ren-ton. The Union Express, northbound (1-down), and the Union Limited, southbound (2-up), were the crack trains of the inter-war years. They were superseded by the first air-conditioned Blue Train just before the outbreak of World War II.

Hex River Pass: Gateway to the Karoo

We're at De Doorns in 1943. Revenue freights, munitions trains and troop specials are crammed into the station and strung out all the way up the valley from Worcester, while Operating tries to slot them into the cavalcade of traffic over the Hex River Pass. In 66 years this bottleneck has never been so busy.

Our train has been impatiently awaiting its turn to tackle the mountain. A four-year-old 23 strains at the leash in front and a 14CR banker with full head of steam is poised 17 coaches back. We're already seven hours late because of wash-aways in the Karoo, and the whole valley of the Hex is in winter drab. Along-

side on tracks 2 and 3 are freights, each with locomotives fore and aft, waiting to follow on behind us.

A trio of 14CRs, returning light from Matroosberg for another round of banking duties, drift in off the main and move on shed. This is our cue. A melancholy whistle from our 23 floats around the valley like a Paul Desmond solo, and with answering crow from the banker we're away in pouring rain. We charge round some tight S-curves out of De Doorns but the 1 in 40 soon bites into our momentum and we settle down to a steady 20 mph.

The sound of the razor-edged exhausts is muted by the misty

drizzle, but the music made by these two giants is a kind of syncopated cha-cha caused by the 15-inch difference in wheel diameter between the 23 and the 14CR. Onwards and upwards, faster on the few straights, slower, with singing flanges, on the curves. Over the saddle into Osplaas we overtake a double-headed string of empty DZs, then winding upwards around the magnificent horseshoe location we thunder into the deep kloof below Tunnel. Suddenly our 23's wheels spin behind a blind blur of rods. The driver shuts her off to control the slip, but with speed slackening to a crawl the trusty banker keeps pushing our 17 coaches, the 23 and all. Speed about 5 mph and falling now, but the front engine regains traction for a few yards to help along before losing it wildly again on the wet rails. From the first coach to the last, heads peer out of open windows, unmindful of the rain, to take in this drama on the mountain. For a few hundred yards we barely keep moving, until the front crew seems to overcome the problem with sand and once more the balancing speed is regained. We have left Osplaas several hundred feet below on the opposite side of the kloof, and the first following freight can be seen just drawing in.

We cross two freights in the level dead-end roads at Tunnel and blast on up the last lap to Matroosberg. Above the Tunnel sidings the unforgettable view down the Hex River Valley rolls out beneath the train. On the right covered in snow is the Matroosberg massif, over 7 000 feet high, backed up by the Buffelshoek range, and on the left are the red sandstone buttresses of the Keeromsberg whose very name – 'turn-about mountain' – conjures up visions of wagon treks abandoned after many days of struggle.

Two miles below Matroosberg the grade eases briefly, causing the wide-open engines to accelerate to a pace which seems much too rapid for the minute 48" wheels of the banker. We sail into the last ramp to the summit and a few minutes later draw into Matroosberg where the banker is detached to turn on the triangle and return to De Doorns. All in a day's work for the 14CR and her crew who have covered these 16 miles thousands of times.

Today, 35 years later, the pass is still there and it is still a bottleneck, but the vital ingredient is missing. For two decades steam has been gone, except for the occasional light engine travelling to or from the workshops at Salt River. The crews of today work their quietly efficient electric units up the mountain with only a fraction of the skill and experience that was needed with steam, and the downhill runs, controlled by regenerative braking, are far easier on brake shoes than were the vacuum-braked descents of old. There can be few other stretches of railway more spectacularly beautiful and more harshly evocative of what we have lost with the passing of the steam locomotive.

18 A glistening Class GMAM No. 4139 brings the Union Express up the valley of the Hex, near Sandhills, on 16 September 1977. To coincide with the last voyage of the last mailship, S.A. Vaal, the RSSA arranged all-steam commemorative runs of the Union Limited and the Union Express. These beautifully organised specials were a huge success and were fully booked months in advance.

The Hex River Pass was opened in 1877. The construction of the 37-mile mountain section with its vertical rise of 2 500 feet from Worcester to the summit had taken two and a half years to complete. Twenty miles on 1 in 66 grade brought the railway up the narrow valley of the Hex to the little town of De Doorns, whose main claim to fame for 80 years was its engine shed housing the bankers for the pass. It took a further 17 miles of heavy engineering on 1 in 40 grade to crest the 3 200-foot summit at Matroosberg.

Until the formation of the South African Railways (SAR) at the time of Union in 1910, no specific engine types were assigned to banking turns. An assortment of early CGR power was used at first, helped in later years by Classes 6 and 8. Soon after Union a batch of Reid Class H tanks arrived at De Doorns and these bore the brunt of banking duties until the early twenties, when Classes MC and MC1 Mallets were drafted in. These powerful machines, with their tractive efforts in excess of 50 000 lbs, survived in mountain service until 1937 when they were replaced by Classes 3B and 14C. The 14Cs, by then re-boilered and classified 14CR, were the last bankers stationed at De Doorns, and when the shed was closed in 1957 they were transferred to the Eastern Cape for service in the Transkei.

19 A 15F banked by a 14CR works northbound empties about two miles below the summit at Matroosberg in 1948. In the background the mountain for which the station is named, the highest in the Western Cape, looms over the train. Note the immaculate track, hand-tamped in the days before mechanisation.

Braking heavy trains down the Hex River Pass required fine judgement, and at intervals on the way down there were notices which said, 'Reduce speed to 15 mph before re-creating vacuum.' The vacuum brake is not the most efficient device for mountain railways, but there have been very few accidents on the pass attributable to loss of brakes. The worst occurred in 1914 when a troop special carrying the Kaffrarian Rifles to Cape Town for embarkation to Europe ran away and overturned about one and a half miles before Tunnel station. Eight soldiers were killed.

20 *Little shed, big mountains.* This unprepossessing structure was home to the Hex River bankers for over 80 years. T. V. Bulpin caught these 14CRs being prepared for banking assignments in 1948. Note the primitive coaling arrangements.

21 A 14CR and 15F double-head goods about two miles above Tunnel station in 1948. This combination of engines was allowed to take 800 tons up the mountain, provided the 14CR was at the rear. When double-heading, they were allowed only 700 tons.

22 Cleaning the extended smokebox of a Class 25.

23 Sunrise on 6 October 1973 found this condenser in full stride with the eastbound Orange Express on its 1 300-mile journey between Cape Town and Durban. The train is nearing Biesiespoort station on a tremendous sweeping curve, part of a line re-location completed in 1942. From here there are less than four miles to go to the 4 560-foot summit, highest point on the Cape Main Line and culmination of the 65-mile bank from Beaufort West.

24 Peter Stow caught this pair of condensers running through ex-Springbok Mannetjies Roux's farm on the 1 in 80 climb to Biesiespoort in November 1973. Double-headed 25s were rated at 1 800 tons on this grade. The old formation, which reached the summit on 1 in 70 uncompensated, is now used as a road at this point and can be seen on the right.

The Great Karoo

Years and years I've trekked across it,
Ridden back and fore,
Till the silence and the glamour
Ruled me to the core;
No man ever knew it better,
None could love it more.
                    Percival Gibbon

Disturbing the silence is a low almost imperceptible whine, far away, swelling with the wind. The sound grows gradually louder as a long caravan crawls towards us over the desert vastness of the Karoo. The whirring of fans and turbines reaches a crescendo as the train passes by, then gradually recedes until a smoky smudge on the horizon is the only evidence of its passing.

The whirring of fans and turbines is the call of the spectacular Class 25 condenser 4-8-4, the last new steam design for the SAR. It utilised its own water eight times over by directing its exhaust steam to the tender instead of into the atmosphere – hence the absence of the traditional chuffing noise. From 1954 these machines began to take over the service between Touws River and De Aar and, once initial teething troubles had been overcome, could show a saving of 90% on water through an area where water supplies had always been a problem.

The territory through which they operated was arid and rugged. From Pieter Meintjies summit, just north of Touws River, the railway meanders mostly downhill through the Koup until at Dwyka trains are back at the level of De Doorns. For southbound

traffic this stretch through the driest region of the Karoo is by far the severest obstacle on the Cape Main Line. The 1 in 60 grade up from Laingsburg through Matjiesfontein, known as the Pieter Meintjies Bank, was the main reason for the decision to electrify from Touws River to Beaufort West in 1959. Northwards from Beaufort West the condensers continued to grind up the 65-mile grade to Biesiespoort until 1974, when the diesel invader finally ousted them from the desert for which they had been designed.

With few exceptions the evolution of motive power through the Karoo followed a predictable pattern, from the earliest CGR engines through Classes 4A, 15A, 15CA and 15E, culminating in the 25s. North of Beaufort West, Pacifics were used from very early on when Beatty's famous 'Karoo' types, the various Classes 5, were introduced from 1903. We are fortunate that two of these magnificent machines, Nos. 723 and 781 (the latter in rebuilt form) have been preserved at De Aar loco. The fine tradition of Pacifics was continued after 1925 by the Baldwin-built 16Ds which worked the passenger links on this section until the outbreak of World War II. Today the original 16D, 'Big Bertha', No. 860, is also preserved at De Aar.

Another famous class which came to be associated with the Beaufort West-De Aar run was the 15E, active here for two decades from 1935. With their poppet valves these Bongols were ideally suited to the fast running required in the Karoo, but their large hand-fired grates precluded them from hauling the Blue Train. An endorsement in the engine-load tables for the period assigned Class 23 to 1-down and 2-up.

25

26

24

25 15Fs, displaced by dieselisation of the Pretoria-Pietersburg line, returned to the Western Cape during 1973 after an absence of 16 years—this time for much humbler duties. On transfer to Cape Town's Paarden Eiland shed, this 15F piloting a 25 made a rare combination, photographed while crossing a northbound goods headed by 3505, ten minutes after sunset at Noblesfontein, November 1973.

26 When electrification to Beaufort West was completed in 1961, the condensers' main field of operation changed over to the long branch westward into the Kalahari from Kimberley. The reason was ore, iron and manganese, which rapidly made the Postmasburg-Sishen-Hotazel line one of the biggest money-spinners on the SAR. Meanwhile the 25NCs which were in operation between Klerksdorp and De Aar began to penetrate condenser territory south to Beaufort West, and for nearly ten years they handled a considerable amount of the traffic exchanged with the *'draadkarre'* (electric units) at Beaufort West. Victor Hand caught this trio of NCs at Beaufort West shed, ready for northbound action one night in August 1965.

27 Locomotive Foreman Alec Watson of De Aar is renowned for his love of steam locomotives. Most of those in his care have girls' names. Here Class 25 NC No. 3434, 'Corry', pilots a condensing 25 southbound from Orange River in August 1977. Within months, the use of condensers on the main line south from Kimberley virtually came to an end. Those that remain are used for shunting work and limited operation north and east from Kimberley.

29 30
31
32
33

De Aar

Ask any railway enthusiast about De Aar, and the chances are he will tell you it is one of the shrines of the steam world. De Aar's main shed – at the southern end of South Africa's busiest steam main line – holds engines awaiting restoration. Every effort is made to restore them to their original condition and they are carefully preserved. However, as our concern is with living steam, we will concentrate on the action at De Aar which within all too short a time will become but a memory.

28 From the front coupler to the tail marker 12 azure-blue and battleship-grey coaches back, this was a train as close to perfection as ever rolled on SAR rails. The new Blue Train may be world-acclaimed, but for many it cannot bear comparison with the original mahogany- and teak-panelled, steam-hauled No. 1-down, seen here thundering into a December dawn north of Modder River in 1971.

29 No. 1547, a beautiful 12A named Stephanie, clears her boiler at the blowdown tunnel.

30 'Milly': smokebox decoration.

31 Numberplate on a preserved 4-6-0.

32 'Milly': cylinder detail.

33 Pride of De Aar is 'Milly', one of two surviving examples of Hendrie's finest design, the 15A.

34 'Ezette' gets some careful grooming before working a northbound passenger train.

Steel Kyalami: De Aar to Kimberley

Nicknamed 'Steel Kyalami' by train crews, after the Grand Prix circuit near Johannesburg, the De Aar-Kimberley line with its relatively straight alignment has long been the race track of the SAR. Speeds over 70 mph were common until a big clamp-down in 1973. The fastest time for this section was set in 1961 when a 25NC hauling one coach and a guard's van made a mercy dash with a severely injured shunter from De Aar to Kimberley. The 147 miles were run in even time, setting a record which is unlikely ever to be bettered.

Today the SAR's last main line still worked by steam has become an attraction for visitors from all over the world. The little lineside hotels at Kraankuil and Witput are often booked up weeks in advance by enthusiasts eager to see maximum horse-power steam in action.

Apart from a few diesel-hauled trains, almost all traffic is handled by 25NCs whose ranks are currently being swelled by the addition of converted condensers. After the Class 25s were released from Karoo service in 1974, the condensing feature with its additional maintenance costs became unnecessary. To bring these 25s into line with their non-condensing sisters, the smokebox turbine and exhauster fan are removed and replaced by a conventional blast pipe. The tender is stripped of the five huge cooling fans, and the small reservoir is replaced by a long, thin 10 000-gallon tank which fits on the original chassis.

35 A converted Class 25 working up the bank to Witput. The bulk of this class has now been rebuilt to match the specifications of the original 25 NC.

36 The last southbound steam-powered Blue Train, with No. 3443 in charge, waters at Orange River in September 1972.

2 Some Western Cape Byways

Over the Hottentots Holland: The Caledon line

Station Master Lodewyk Frans Geldenhuys is worried. His station, Sir Lowry's Pass, is full of trains and there's another at the home signal. The first driver scheduled out has already had the tablet for 15 minutes, while he strives to put a bit of life into the fire of No. 4001, a GEA suffering from years of mechanical neglect.

It is mid-March 1975. The fruit season is in full swing and the apple farmers at Elgin, on the far side of the Hottentots Holland Mountains, are clamouring for empties. But the GEAs, with less than a year to live, can show only a shadow of their former capabilities and are creating nightmares for the operating staff.

At long last 4001 whistles up and rumbles out of the yard with her rake of the sought-after O-type trucks. Her place at the mountainside water column is taken immediately by No. 4019 heading another batch of empties, and the main is thus cleared for an opposing load of apples to depart for Cape Town.

It is 1 100 vertical feet up to the summit tunnel along nine miles of track, but 4001 covers barely a third of the distance before leaking elements and weary valve rings take their toll and it is time to stop for a blow-up. Twenty minutes go by before the water

is again at the top of the glass and the needle of the pressure gauge reaches the red line at 200 lbs. Even with an empty train, restarting on the 1 in 40 uncompensated gradient calls for considerable skill on the part of the crew. But with the help of some sand, the 16 steel drivers bite into the rails and for another three miles 4001 trudges on before giving up the ghost.

By this time the healthier beat of 4019 can be heard leaving Sir Lowry's Pass. Within 20 minutes she is exploding the detonators which protect 4001's rear as she draws cautiously up to the guard's van. With much whistling and crashing of slack the two trains combine and start for the summit, an impressive lash-up of 50 wagons and two Garratts.

37 Negotiating the narrow rocky defile of Houhoek Pass, a GEA heads the 7.15 am Caledon-Cape Town weekday goods in July 1975.

38 During the fruit season Garratts were often in short supply, and the stalwart 14CRBs were used as back-up power. Here in March 1974 No. 1888 is working empties up Sir Lowry's Pass, with the Hottentots Holland Range in the background.

37 38

Meanwhile Station Master Geldenhuys is on the 'phone to Station Foreman Heyns at Elgin, explaining what has delayed the empties. The ageing GEAs are sitting down on the mountain almost every day now, causing chaos on the line. 'Looks like it's going to be a rough season this year,' says the harassed Geldenhuys. 'I think we'll just manage the Golden Delicious and the Winter Pearmains, but we'll never make it with the Granny Smiths.'

Ever since the railway reached Caledon in 1902 the operation of this mountainous line has created problems. Double-heading and banking were often resorted to, and from early on a considerable number of classes were used, from early CGR hand-me-downs to Garratts, and some of the first types specifically designed for branch lines, the 19As and 19Bs. The GDs worked here for a few years until 1935 when they were replaced by poppet-valved 19Cs which were so successful that their sharp relentless bark could be heard in the mountains until the end of steam at Caledon in 1976. Up to the mid-sixties when the GEAs were drafted in, the 19Cs were the standard power, although there were often exceptions to the general pattern, with Classes 1, 6, 8 and particularly 14CRB helping out.

Two unusual engines associated with this route were 'Takbok' (No. 2456) and 'Renoster' (No. 4009). In 1967 in an attempt to eliminate spark-throwing in the Western Cape wheatlands they were fitted with extended horizontal chimneys with turned-up ends (illustrated opposite). At the time A. E. Durrant commented aptly in *The Continental Railway Journal*: 'These tubes [the chimneys] apparently contain nothing in the way of baffles or netting, and it is presumably hoped that the sparks will simply die of fright while traversing the long dark passages!'

The man responsible for these experiments was the Assistant Locomotive Superintendent at Cape Town, Johannes Barnard, brother of the famous heart surgeons. For years he had concerned himself with the prevention of lineside fires which annually cost the SAR large amounts in claims from farmers. He had previously developed a fairly successful type of smokebox spark arrestor, but Takbok and Renoster were the culmination of his efforts to find a lasting solution to the problem. The experiments were said to be successful, but they were never repeated and the weird chimneys were removed shortly after Mr Barnard retired in 1971.

Sir Lowry's Pass

39 Many combinations of engines have been used to heave traffic over the Hottentots Holland, but double-headed GEAs were extremely rare.

40 A view of No. 4009, 'Renoster' (rhinoceros), from her cab roof showing her as she was in 1971. When running forward, she looked very much like a charging rhinoceros.

41 An old Class 8DW, No. 1208, assists 14CRB No. 1767 with empties bound for Elgin during the 1969 fruit season. The 'W' indicates that the 8th Class was fitted with long-travel piston valves during the Watson regime – a conversion which considerably increased their effectiveness and gave them their characteristic razor-sharp exhaust beat.

42 With a full load of fruit, Class 19C No. 2456, 'Takbok' (reindeer), pulls out of Sir Lowry's Pass station bound for the pre-cooling sheds at Cape Town.

43 A pair of 14CRBs brings empty FZ trucks up the western side of the pass in April 1974.

Moving the apples:
Seasonal traffic from Elgin

About March the markets of London are piled high with boxes of Cape apples. The chances are that they will have come from Elgin, and until very recently they would have begun their 6 000-mile journey behind steam. The aroma of ripe apples mixed with steam and smoke used to hang over the Elgin valleys between February and May each year as various combinations of Garratt and non-articulated engines struggled to get their cargoes over the mountain and down to the export pre-coolers at Cape Town docks. There was not much time: from picking to pre-cooling was supposed to take no more than 24 hours, and this meant a continual procession of trains over Sir Lowry's Pass. At the height of the season an average of 140 loads was cleared each day, over and above regular traffic. In flat country this might not have been much of a feat, but out of Elgin a solid five miles of 1 in 40 uncompensated faces westbound traffic, and the working of steam on this section over this grade was spectacular.

44 A 14CR and a GEA stand in the yard at Elgin, ready to depart. About half a mile ahead is the Palmiet River Bridge, where the five-mile twisting grade of 1 in 40 begins. During the fruit season nearly all trains were assisted between Elgin and Steenbras. For many years this was done by banking, generally with a 14CR, but double-heading was resorted to during 1974 and 1975, the last two years of steam over the mountain.

45 19 loads and a van add up to 900 tons of train, sufficient to bring this 14CR and GEA down to walking pace on the bank from Elgin to Steenbras. Long after they had passed, the scent of freshly-picked apples lingered on.

45

46 For five exciting days in April 1975, enthusiasts were treated to a rare sight: a rotary-cam poppet-valved 19C No. 2438 piloting the Garratts on fruit blocks up to Steenbras. This occurred when the regular 14CRB banker failed and had to be replaced by the 19C off a passing wayside freight.

47 No. 1132, an 8B beautifully painted in something approaching CGR livery at the suggestion of members of the Cape Town branch of the RSSA, is seen here on the horseshoe curve below Steenbras with an RSSA special on Kruger Day, 10 October 1973. As an ex-CSAR engine, she was originally painted black with polished brass dome, boiler bands and driving-wheel splashers, but she looks a picture in green.

48 Station Foreman Heyns flags a charging GEA into Elgin, April 1974.

49 The cannon-blast exhaust of a 14CRB above the inexorable rumble of a GEA was part of fruit-train operation over Sir Lowry's Pass. The perfectly orchestrated sounds ricochetted off the trees, providing tape-recording enthusiasts with some incomparable reels.

Into the Ruggens: Langhoogte

Secondary railways at the southern tip of Africa are characterized by their penetration of the fold mountain ranges of the Western Cape. The branches fall into two categories: those built purely as feeders to main lines, such as those to Franschhoek, Prince Alfred Hamlet, Porterville and Bredasdorp; and the ones originally proposed as through lines and never completed, to Protem, Bitterfontein and Ladismith. In this chapter we have concentrated on the last three because they are typical of lines in the area and are the most interesting in terms of motive power and the variety of countryside through which they pass.

Construction of the Protem and Bitterfontein lines stopped in the middle of nowhere. A glance at the map prompts the question why. A railway through Caledon would appear to offer the quickest passage between Cape Town and Mossel Bay, and if the 30-mile gap between Protem and Swellendam had been closed the route would have been 20 miles shorter. But this shorter route would have been slower, for it is considerably more mountainous. It would have involved crossing four watersheds of over 1 000 feet for a total climb of 3 500 feet, as against half that for the longer way down the Breede River Valley.

50 This GEA has just crossed the bridge at Mission and is winding up for the Langhoogte bank up to Die Vlei. All around, the summer's wheat has been harvested and the silos of the 'ruggens' are filling, to disgorge their contents later in the year as fast as the GEAs can clear the traffic.

51 The same scene in winter, with a GEA bringing FZ trucks to clear the summer's harvest. Rimmed by the snow-covered Riviersonderend Mountains to the north, the 'ruggens' region lies between the Bot and Breede Rivers. The name means 'backs' and refers to the high rounded hills separated by 1 000-foot-deep valleys, which have been a severe hindrance to railway operation in the area. Because of the difficulty of this terrain, coupled with the crossing of the Hottentots Holland Mountains, the railway through Caledon was never extended to Swellendam, which was the original intention. The name Protem ('in the meantime') was given to the present terminus because it was thought that the line would be continued within a few years.

51 50

52

53

52 When Pauling & Co. laid down the formation of the Caledon line through Houhoek Pass, they were forced to span the river in two places, and these two bridges have been well photographed over the years. Here a 14CRB works a freight from Caledon to Cape Town over the lower bridge, the more spectacular of the two, in April 1974.

53 No. 4039 tackles the 1 in 40 of Langhoogte with the 7.15 am Caledon-Cape Town goods, July 1975.

54 'Renoster' without her 'horns'. In April 1974, GEA No. 4009 crossed the Bot River, some 18 months after having her experimental chimney removed. This bridge marks the beginning of the climb through Houhoek Pass – and 25 miles of heavy steaming to crest the Hottentots Holland at Steenbras summit.

55 Class 7A No. 1011 gallops up the last mile into Ladismith with the 'Makadas' in May 1971. The local people use this name for the daily mixed from Touws River – one theory is that it is a corruption of the words 'make a dash'. The mountains rising to over 7 000 feet in the background are the Swartberg, with the cleft peak of Towerkop ('magic peak') visible from over 100 miles away on a clear day.
The Ladismith branch was once intended to be linked with Calitzdorp and Oudtshoorn to give the SAR leverage in a rates dispute with the New Cape Central Railway (see Chapter 3). The link would have cut the private company's share of Cape Town-Port Elizabeth traffic but would have been expensive to construct because the 40-mile gap involved crossing the Huis River Pass. The plan was dropped when the Government took over the NCCR in 1925.

North to Namaqualand

The Bitterfontein railway was intended to reach the Namaqualand towns of Springbok and Okiep to tap some of the traffic generated by the Cape Copper Company. However, the Company had its own 2′ 6″-gauge railway to Port Nolloth, and sent most of its traffic that way. By 1943 it became cheaper for the Company (by then an American concern) to send its ingots by road to the railhead at Bitterfontein, 289 miles from Cape Town. Thus the SAR's Namaqualand railway was never extended and the narrow gauge to Port Nolloth was closed after 75 years of service to the Copper Belt.

56 A pair of 19Cs battle upgrade from Malmesbury with freight for Klawer and beyond.

57 The ripening wheat of the Swartland had little to fear from the 19Cs with their well-maintained spark arresters. Here is No. 2467 just north of Eendekuil in September 1975.

58 A few 19Cs acquired Vanderbilt tenders from the 1948 order of 19Ds. They were mainly used in the arid country north of Klawer. The last water was at Lutzville on the Olifants River and from there they worked to the terminus at Bitterfontein and back without re-watering. Short-tendered 19Cs working north of Klawer were obliged to tow along an extra water tank. Occasionally long-tendered 19Cs came south of Klawer and this one is shown about three miles north of Het Kruis in September 1975.

59 A 16D at Kalbaskraal with a Malmesbury-Cape Town goods train in 1971. Even after their removal from Cape Main Line service in 1939, they continued to do wonderful work on local passenger trains in the Western Cape for another 30 years. Towards the end they were more often found in freight service, but at the time when they were withdrawn these venerable Baldwins were performing with as sprightly a gait as when they were unwrapped from their Yankee packing crates.

60 The Klawer mail was the smartest train left to Cape Western steam after electrification of the main line. For many years the regular performers on the point were Class 15BRs, like the one shown here leaving

Klipheuwel for Malmesbury, from where double-headed 19Cs would take over for the night run to Namaqualand.

61 Coming south from Kalbaskraal is a 15F on the afternoon mixed from Malmesbury, July 1975.

62 North of Eendekuil, 19C No. 2471 approaches Het Kruis with general merchandise for Klawer in December 1975. Note the well-ballasted track which had recently been relaid with 96-lb material. It was promptly dubbed *'die teerpad'* (the tarred road) by footplatemen accustomed to the bone-shaking corrugations in the old 60-lb rails.

3 The Garden Route

Along the Langeberg

Tugging her 13 squealing coaches by sheer brute force, 9-down's GEA struggles out of the Gouritz River Gorge up a series of 5-chain reverse curves. With the skill of years on the footplate, Mickey Gerber closes the regulator as his charge loses her feet, then opens it again, the cut-off marker of the Hadfield reverser away in the corner. The fireman is down on the ballast, walking ahead of the train to shovel sand onto damp morning rails. Dominating all is the ear-ringing percussion as each exhaust beat crashes back off vertical rock cuttings. At last, a gradient post: 1 in 40 to 1 in 66. Driver Gerber squirts a stream of tobacco juice at the post as the fireman swings aboard, the quickening exhaust signalling another battle won. 'If they showed the real gradient on that post we'd never get out of here', he shouts, and on we head for Mossel Bay.

The last major privately-owned and -operated railway in South Africa, the New Cape Central Railway (NCCR), was absorbed by the SAR in 1925. The NCCR was formed in 1894 to take over the assets of the bankrupt Cape Central Railway which ran from

Worcester to Ashton, and to extend it to Voorbaai near Mossel Bay. A Government subsidy of £2 000 per mile was payable on completion of the work, on condition certain standards were met. One of these was that the ruling grade should be no steeper than 1 in 40. The story goes that several stretches were actually steeper than this on the NCCR but the gradient posts were painted as 1 in 40 to satisfy the Government inspectors. Hence driver Gerber's scepticism about the posts at Gouritz River. In fact, the gradients *are* steeper than they appear because they are uncompensated for curvature; the numerous 5-chain curves make the 1 in 40 equivalent to 1 in 33.

9-down normally crosses the Langeberg after dark, but night travel has its compensations on this line. While passing remote halts like Klaasvoogds, Jubilee and Leeurivier, you can lie on the middle bunk watching the coach lights like a string of beads round the curves. As you listen to the Garratt tearing into the grades you catch a whiff of the 'NCCR smell' given off by a variety of the buchu herb, now and then spiced with coal smoke. It is

with you all the way from Worcester to Mossel Bay, and even beyond to Oudtshoorn.

The entire 205 miles of the old NCCR had to be located along the foothills of the Langeberg which resulted in a continuous switch-back profile, almost invariably at ruling grade. This is ideal country for articulated locomotives and indeed Garratts have been associated with the Garden Route for over 50 years.

Until 1923 the NCCR relied almost entirely on 4-8-0s to handle its road services. By that time the prospering company was able to afford two Garratts from Beyer Peacock, and a healthy stable of reliable engines was taken over by the SAR in 1925.

After the takeover the SAR began a re-railing programme, replacing the NCCR's 45-lb rails with 60-lb material, and soon after the new Gouritz River Bridge was completed in 1931 it was possible to replace all the old NCCR stalwarts with Class 14Cs. The 30-year monopoly of the magnificent 7s had come to an end, but as SAR Classes 7E and 7F they were to see duty for many more years on the Touws River-Ladismith and other branches. The GKs were transferred to Natal's Underberg branch where they gave good service until the sixties.

The 14Cs thus became sole power on the line until they in turn were challenged by the GEAs from 1947 onwards. In 1958 the GEAs were supplanted as far as Riversdale by GMAs (nicknamed 'Gammats'), and only in 1975 to Mossel Bay and beyond. In recent years even 15BRs and 15Fs have appeared along the Langeberg, the 15Fs only as far as Ashton.

63 In September 1971, Train 51-down with a GMAM in charge on its once-weekly run between the Mother City and Algoa Bay, winds through the wheatfields near Jubilee. In the background the sandstone krantzes of the Leeurivierberg glow in the evening light. This express has now been discontinued, and alien traction threatens scenes like these throughout the Garden Route.

64 With fire stoked and ready for the heavy climb out of the Gouritz Valley, a GEA takes 9-down across the river in April 1973. The old bridge once shared by NCCR trains with road traffic can be seen behind the new one. At 208 feet above mean water level the new bridge was the highest on the SAR's 3' 6" gauge until 1973 when the magnificent arches were completed over the White Umfolozi on the Richards Bay line.

The Knysna Branch

65 A Class 24 accelerates away from the Kaaimans River, heading for Victoria Bay with the morning mixed from Knysna to George. This branch has some of the finest railway scenery in South Africa and could become a major tourist attraction. As it is now, people can enjoy a day's outing from either the George or Knysna end and more and more holidaymakers are patronising it during the season. But it must be allowed to continue with steam traction: overseas experience has shown that diesels do not attract tourists to this sort of railway.

66 The same train is seen earlier crossing the vlei at Sedgefield.

66

65

Montagu Pass

Bertram Lewis recalls a night journey over the Outeniquas in about 1920 when he was a schoolboy:

'I awoke at a quarter to eleven to find that we were commencing the ascent of the Outeniquas. Within a minute I was dressed and out on the balcony of the coach, looking down on a stretch of wild, lonely coast with enormous waves brilliantly lit by the moon. Every inch of this sharply-curved line was impressive, with its huge dark dongas, tunnel and high concrete embankment.

When we reached George, where the ritual of grate cleaning, coal trimming and taking water was performed, I could see that our two locomotives were Class 8s and the train consisted of 12 balcony saloons which were of course lighter than modern stock.

The climb up Montagu Pass started immediately out of George – an easy 1 in 100 at first, rising to 1 in 80 as we wound among huge planted trees, then past indigenous forest where the lilac flowers of the keurboom gleamed. After the horseshoe curve, where the train reversed direction, the real climbing began, with the gradient continuously 1 in 36, easing to 1 in 48 for the sharper curves. It was almost painful to hear the engines straining.

Far below I could see the lights of George and Mossel Bay, while not far above the mountainside was thickly covered in snow; but the immediate prospect now was a contrast of softly illuminated grass- and fern-covered slopes, and ominous dark ravines. The more we climbed the wilder it became, until we turned into a deep ravine shortly after the first tunnel and stopped for ten minutes to service the engines at the remote Power siding. I know of no more romantic place. Just a few hundred yards ahead the line plunged through the blackness almost to the floor of the kloof, where it turned sharply left into a tunnel and emerged a hundred feet above the siding.

67

68

69

After Power we seemed to be in the very bowels of the mountain and the dark cuttings and tunnels gave a thrill to a small boy which is with him still. Gradually we turned into the huge amphitheatre below Cradock Peak, then the vertical concrete embankment gave way to a high arched viaduct and suddenly we were in the tunnel at the top of the pass where the siding in those days was called 'Summit'. Outside there was snow all around and even lower down at Camfer the ground was still white.

The train ran double-headed all the way, and I was told that the only way the engine crews could survive in the tunnels was to cover their faces with wet cloths and to lie on the floor of the cab. Later, when the neat little GD Garratts worked this line, the procedure was to run double-headed from Mossel Bay to George, and then the front engine, usually an 8th Class, ran to the back of the train and banked it to the summit.'

67 *'Into the bowels of the mountain'*. Having crossed its opposite number, 9-down's GEA wrenches its train out of the tunnel in the ravine above Power siding – a sight once seen never forgotten. Note the angle of the 1 in 36 grade that this articulated is working with a 14-coach long-distance sleeping- and dining-car express. With the earlier GDs it was the practice to bank up from George if the load exceeded 10 coaches. A single GEA was rated at 560 tons up the mountain as compared with 400 tons for a GD. In the foreground, 8-up sits out the compulsory ten-minute stop for downhill trains to cool brakeshoes.

68 This is how it looked at Power in the twenties, when Bertram Lewis made his first trip over the pass. A downhill train is standing at the mountainside water column, headed by a Class 8 and a Belpaire-boilered Class 6.

69 *'The more we climbed, the wilder it became'*. The coastal plateau and the town of George have been left far, far below as the Mossel Bay-Johannesburg express drawn by a GEA approaches the huge ravine below Power.

The line from Mossel Bay to Klipplaat must surely rank with the most beautiful in the world, for it crosses the Outeniqua Mountains and the Little Karoo, one of the loveliest regions in South Africa. It was built in stages from both ends, construction commencing in 1898. The Mossel Bay team reached George by 1907, and this section was worked by the NCCR under an agreement with the CGR. Meanwhile on the other side of the Outeniquas the plate-layers reached Oudtshoorn in 1904.

Between the coastal plateau and the Little Karoo lay the formidable barrier of the Outeniquas, and there was only one way through – Montagu Pass. Construction proceeded slowly while eight tunnels and numerous cuttings were blasted through solid rock on a grade of 1 in 36 compensated. In 1913 the link between George and Oudtshoorn was at last completed, providing a direct rail link between Cape Town and Port Elizabeth, though 'direct' is perhaps an overstatement. Since 1884 a link between these two cities had existed via De Aar – a distance of 830 miles. Via Mossel Bay the rail distance is 675 miles, compared with 410 air miles.

NCCR locomotives were used as far as George until Montagu Pass was opened. The agreement with the CGR was then terminated, and the CGR's engines began to work through from Klipplaat. Classes 6, 7 and 8 were used at random right down the line. Double-heading over the pass was common and this led to experiments with articulated machines towards the end of the twenties. Classes FC and FD (the so-called 'modified Fairlies') as well as GE and GD were tried, but only the GDs established themselves. For 20 years they were the main power over the Outeniquas but it still took two of them to move the mail train over the mountain, and it was not until the advent of the GEAs in 1947 that one engine was able to do the job.

In 1975 began what will probably be the final chapter in the story of steam over the Montagu Pass for it was then that GMAs, displaced by dieselization in Natal arrived at Voorbaai, and by the end of the year they were handling all trains between Riversdale and Oudtshoorn.

70 High above the cloud banks rolling in from the Indian Ocean, a GEA nears tunnel 6 with a special for fruit-pickers returning to the Longkloof orchards after the Easter weekend, 1974.

71 One hour out from George and 1 000 feet higher, it's time for a drink at Power.

72 A GMAM approaches Oupad on its way up the northern slopes of Montagu Pass in January 1977.

73 8-up drifts downhill through tunnel 5, April 1974.

74 This GMAM No. 4127 on a goods for Mossel Bay still has 200 feet to climb to Topping as it leaves Oupad in January 1977. It has just climbed through the only area in South Africa where hops can be grown successfully.

The Little Karoo

Sudden the desert changes,
   The red glare softens and clings,
Till the aching Oudtshoorn ranges,
   Stand up like the thrones of kings.

Royal the pageant closes,
   Lit by the last of the sun –
Opal and ash-of-roses,
   Cinnamon, umber and dun.

We hear the Hottentot herders
   As the sheep click past to the fold,
And the crick of the restless girders
   As the steel contracts in the cold.

Voices of jackals calling,
   And, loud in the hush between,
A morsel of dry earth falling
   From the flanks of the scarred ravine.

And the solemn firmament marches,
   And the hosts of heaven rise,
Framed through the iron arches,
   Banded and barred by the ties.

Till we feel the far track humming,
   And we see her headlight plain,
And we gather and wait her coming, –
   The wonderful northbound train.

Rudyard Kipling

As a geographical region, the Little Karoo begins around Camfer,
but in spirit it begins near Oudtshoorn. It is a land of vermilion
cliffs, green fields of lucerne and strutting ostriches, wild flowers
of every hue, little white-washed thatched Cape cottages, and
grand Victorian-Edwardian farmhouses built during the great
ostrich feather boom.

75 *'Lit by the last of the sun.'* Soon the swift twilight of the desert will
give way to night and the headlight of No. 3334 will illuminate the rails
east of Rooiloop.

76

76 For nearly 30 years the Vanderbilt-tendered 3321-series 19Ds have been associated with the Oudtshoorn-Klipplaat run. Here No. 3323 crosses a southbound special passenger train which has just emerged from Toorwaterpoort (behind the train), April 1977.

77 Even today ostrich farming is an important industry in the Little Karoo: 3337 heading 9-down passes nonchalant pairs of breeding birds near Stompdrift, January 1977.

78 A string of mechanical refrigerators with fresh fish for the dorps of the Highveld; near Barandas, January 1977.

77

79 Near Snyberg, the tremendous red wall of eggo-conglomerate – perfectly rounded river pebbles set in a matrix of finer material – towers over the eastbound Port Elizabeth mail just before sunset, December 1973.

Lootsberg Pass

Northwards from Graaff-Reinet the railway exploits the course of the Sundays River through Pretoriuskloof and the southern ramparts of the Sneeuberg to reach the 5 727-foot summit of Lootsberg Pass. To gain altitude the surveyors were forced to locate along every curve of the river, for tunnels or bridges would have increased the grade unacceptably. In spite of severe curvature some lively running could be experienced in the days of the 19Bs.

Most memorable for us was a run on 1300-up, the Mossel Bay-Johannesburg express. We embarked at Graaff-Reinet and were 45 minutes late in leaving. Up front in double harness was a 24 leading a 19B. Oom Tollie Nel of Rosmead was at the throttle of the pilot engine and it was soon apparent that he was bent on

getting home on time. We entered the tortuous gorge of the Sundays just when delicious smells began wafting back from the kitchen car. The engines roared around the curves at such a rate that centrifugal force obliged us to hold tight – or be ejected through the carriage windows! All very exhilarating – and by Pretoriuskloof we had made up ten minutes.

Here 1300 stopped for water, and as we watched a brawny man in a white chef's hat alighted from the kitchen car and marched down the cinder path towards the engines. He went straight to Oom Tollie who was busy greasing around, and an angry pantomime followed. Just when fisticuffs seemed inevitable, the driver of the 19B whistled up for departure. Oom Tollie

80 81 82

80 Working on a southbound goods, two 19Bs, Nos. 1405 and 1410, lift maximum tonnage (600 tons for the two engines) up the pass in May 1971. They have just taken pure untreated mountain water at Jagpoort and are ascending a tilted plain between two spurs of the Sneeuberg, up which the railway describes a sinuous path to maintain the 1 in 40 ruling grade.

81 To make up for the sparse passenger service on country lines, SAR goods trains often have passenger accommodation – witness one satisfied customer.

82 Double-headed 19Bs on Train 1305, the Johannesburg-Mossel Bay express, about three miles from the summit in July 1974. When the Lootsberg route was opened in 1898, the ubiquitous Class 7s became the mainstay of the mountain section, but in the early twenties they were supplemented by Class 8s. In the thirties the 19Bs began an association with this route which was to last for over 40 years. Classes 6, 8, 19D and 24 also put in a lot of work, but the 19Bs always predominated. They had a loud square beat which woke the echoes of the mountains in a haunting way.

83 The swirling mists of dawn hide the rocky cockscomb of the Sneeuberg behind this special southbound train for American railway enthusiasts in September 1975. There is still a mile to go to Lootsberg, from where the front 19D will continue with the train down the long descent to Klipplaat. The Class 24 banker will be detached at the summit and turned on the triangle before returning to Rosmead.

84 For many decades 6th Class engines were used for shunting, banking and pilot work, and one regular 6th Class turn was the fortnightly washout working to Rosmead. The Graaff-Reinet shunter invariably ran double-headed over the mountain. Here the very last such working leaves Blouwater in March 1970 with No. 454 piloting Class 24 No. 3617. No. 454 had recently emerged from shops and was in perfect mechanical condition, but after this trip she scarcely turned a wheel before being sent to De Aar for preservation.

85 The Nels take a train through Pretoriuskloof. Tollie Nel of Rosmead shed, with his regular 1410 (the only Class 19BR engine) pilots Jimmie 'Bosbokkie' Nel in his 1412 near Willow Slopes in September 1973.

boarded his 24, with a clang of the tender lids we were under way, and the chef had to scramble aboard the moving train. There was no soup for lunch, but we got to Rosmead on time!

For many years the Rosmead 19Bs (and even the 24s) worked a diagram which involved through running between Klipplaat and Noupoort. From Kendrew there is a continuous ramp of 84 miles to Lootsberg summit with a vertical climb of 3 712 feet, followed by a descent to Rosmead and another climb of 1 180 feet in 21 miles to the continental divide at Carlton.

Hand-firing an engine up nearly 5 000 feet in one day is a feat which should qualify Rosmead firemen for an entry in *The Guinness Book of Records* – especially when one remembers that the coal was frequently of poor quality, and the 19Bs, although beautifully sure-footed machines for the mountains, had short-travel valves and voracious appetites.

Once we rode the footplate of No. 1413 on a northbound freight out of Graaff-Reinet. At 330 tons we were 15 tons overloaded for the 1 in 40 grades, and with driver Strauss in charge we knew we were in for an interesting ride.

The first four miles are solid 1 in 40 against the engine and we barely held walking pace. In spite of a huge build-up of 1413's fire before the 'right away', the young fireman was soon shovelling hard, sweat running down his neck. There was to be no respite for him for over four hours, except at the water stops at Pretoriuskloof and Koloniesplaas. At Blouwater, where the last 1 000 feet to the summit begins, driver Strauss casually reached into his seat box and pulled out a wedge-shaped chunk of ballast which he jammed into the regulator quadrant. This held the lever full open against the vibration of the engine. Seeing our surprise when the fireman collapsed onto his seat and he grabbed the shovel, the driver shouted above the roar of the exhaust, *'Ek stook maar die berg uit.'* There was apparently an understanding amongst some Rosmead crews that the last nine miles to the summit should be fired by the drivers.

This tradition ended with the arrival on the Lootsberg route of GMAM Garratts in 1976. With their mechanical stokers they should have cut down on the work of the firemen, but at this time the SAR took delivery of some of the worst coal it had ever used which meant that firemen spent almost as much time cleaning fire as they had previously spent shovelling.

Winter on Lootsberg

86 The first sitting for lunch is in full swing in the snug dining car of Train 1300. Outside it is well below freezing as 19B No. 1413, in her last year of service, pilots an unidentified 19D up the south slope of Lootsberg

4 Midland Rails

Port Elizabeth Locals

Few services in South Africa can claim to have enjoyed a century of steam operation. One of the few is the Port Elizabeth-Uitenhage service where steam trains began operations in 1875. Today this is the last steam suburban railway in South Africa.

It was in this service that Classes 10A and 10B established themselves after the Witwatersrand electrification displaced them in the thirties. All but two were rebuilt with the Watson standard boiler into Class 10BR, but all retained the long-lap,

long-travel valves with which they were built in 1910. It was the latter feature which enabled them to perform with such zest on the 11-coach Uitenhage sets. With over 300 tons behind the tender they ran the 21 miles in under 50 minutes with eight intermediate stops, accelerating up to 60 mph between stations.

These small engines endured a thrashing for over 60 years, an extraordinary testimony to the durability of G. G. Elliot's design. He was the last Chief Mechanical Engineer of the Central South

		206	210	208	232	212	220	226	214	216	218	222	224	228	236	248	240	258	262	266	270	272	274 B	278	276 A	254 D	246	284	282	260 B	288	292	294	290	308	242	295	298
PORT ELIZABETH....(LR)..	V	5 15	5 20	5 35	6 0	6 6	6 15	6 34	6 45	6 56	7 5	7 35	8 25	9 45	11 30	12 55	1 30	2 20	3 45	4 8	4 37	4 42	4 56	5 5	5 10	5 15	5 33	5 38	5 43	5 55	6 15	7 7	7 38	8 10	8 15	9 30	10 10	11 35
North End	"	5 18	5 23	5 38	6 3	6 9	6 18	6 37	6 48	6 59	7 8	7 38	8 28	9 48	11 33	12 58	1 33	2 23	3 48	4 11	4 40	4 45	4 59	5 8	5 13	5 18	5 36	5 41	5 46	5 58	6 18	7 10	7 41	8 13	8 21	9 33	10 13	11 38
Sydenham ....(LR)..	"	5 23	5 28	5 43	6 8	6 14	6 23	6 42	6 53	7 4	7 13	7 43	8 33	9 53	11 38	1 3	1 38	2 28	3 53	4 16	4 45	4 50	5 4	5 13	5 18	5 24	5 42	5 46	5 51	5 58	6 22	7 15	7 46	8 18	8 27	9 38	10 18	11 43
New Brighton	"	5 28	5 33	5 48	6 13	6 19	6 28	6 47	6 58	7 9	7 18	7 48	8 38	9 58	11 43	1 8	1 43	2 33	3 58	4 21	4 50	4 55	5 9	5 18	5 23	5 29	5 47	5 51	5 56	6 3	6 27	7 20	7 51	8 23	8 33	9 43	10 23	11 49
Swartkops	"		5 39	5 54	6 19		6 34			7 15			8 43		11 49	1 13		2 39	4 4	4 27		5 1	5 15		5 29	5 36		5 57	6 1		6 32		7 57		8 41		10 28	11 54
Redhouse	"			6 1			6 44			7 24			8 49		11 54	1 19		2 46		4 33		5 6			5 35	5 49		6 4			6 37		8 3		8 49		10 34	11 59
Perserverance	"			6 7			6 49			7 30			8 55		12 0	1 28		2 52		4 39		5 12			5 41	5 55		6 10			6 43		8 9		8 58		10 39	12 4
Despatch	"			6 14			6 56			7 37			9 1		12 7	1 35		2 59		4 46		5 19			5 47	6 5		6 17			6 50		8 16		9 6		10 45	12 11
De Mist.	"			6 24			7 20			7 52			9 8		12 13	1 41		3 5		4 52		5 30			5 55	6 26		6 56			6 56		8 24		9 14		10 52	12 16
UITENHAGE	A			6 28			7 25			7 52			9 12		12 18	1 46		3 10		4 57		5 34			6 1	6 17		6 30			7 1		8 28		9 20		10 57	12 23

African Railways before its incorporation into the SAR in 1910, and the first CME to introduce modern cylinder design to South Africa.

In 1969, 10BRs were superseded by Classes 16R and CR from the Natal South Coast which were destined to be the last Pacifics in passenger service on the SAR. They were retired during 1975, and today the service is handled almost entirely by Class 15ARs.

Though perhaps not as sprightly as their Pacific predecessors, they nevertheless turn in daily performances which would have gladdened the heart of their designer, D. A. Hendrie. When he supervised the completion of the detailed drawings for this fine class over 65 years ago, he could hardly have foreseen that in 1978 some 118 of the original 127 locomotives would still be working. During the late thirties and forties most were rebuilt with Watson standard boilers into Class 15AR. They are equally at home in suburban, shunting, and main-line goods or passenger service – the true maid-of-all-work of the SAR.

87 A classic suburban engine leaves Port Elizabeth for Uitenhage with a classic suburban train in January 1960. For over 30 years the standard formation was a 10 BR Pacific (in this case, No. 760) and a rake of period side-door stock. The 10BRs were invariably kept immaculate by their regular crews, and for several years No. 760, based on Uitenhage shed, was the shiniest. She carried a cast brass plaque reading 'Uitenhage, the Garden Town' under her headlight. Sadly, she was the first 10BR to go when she cracked her frame and was withdrawn during 1962.

88 In her 50th year of service, Class 10B No. 752 drifts into Port Elizabeth under the old signal gantry which disappeared with the rebuilding of the station during the early sixties. Only two of Elliot's 10B Pacifics escaped rebuilding with Watson standard boilers (the other was No. 757), but they were certainly not inferior to the rebuilds in performance.

The 10Bs started their lives in 1910 in express passenger service between Johannesburg, Kimberley and Bloemfontein. When trains became too heavy during the twenties they were relegated to Witwatersrand local passenger work, and after electrification of the Reef services in 1938 they came to the Cape Midland System where their shapely profile and loud bark were part of the scene for another quarter century.

89 A 15AR on a Uitenhage train in full flight near New Brighton. Today almost the entire Uitenhage service is handled by these venerable machines.

90 The nameplate attached unofficially to 15AR No. 2011 by her regular crew.

91 Class 15AR No. 2011 panned at over 50 mph between Redhouse and Swartkops.

92 In the winter of '76 a steamy wedge of a 15AR runs towards Swartkops as fast as her Hendrie front-end will allow.

93 A 10BR spins along near Swartkops in 1971. Even after they were displaced from the suburban trains, the 10BRs continued to do useful work on local freights in the Algoa Bay area.

94 Drifting down towards Despatch on an evening Uitenhage-P.E. local is Class 12AR No. 1545. The use of these muscle-bound machines on the locals was by no means uncommon. Although the 10BRs (and later the Hendrie Pacifics) worked most trains, any power was likely to be called during rush hour. During the last 15 years the following classes have been observed on these trains: 10, 10B, 10BR, 11, 12R, 12AR, 15A, 15AR, 15F, 16R, 16CR, 19B, 19D and 24.

95 All over South Africa there were stations whose importance derived not from service to a nearby community but rather from their location at the start of a long climb into the mountains. Of these fascinating places, only a handful are left: the others have lost their status, ignored by the intruders that now storm past their doors.
Glenconnor, at the foot of the Kleinpoort bank, between Uitenhage and Klipplaat, is one of the few that remain. Here in January 1975, the engines of 8-up have stopped for water, a greasing all round and a fire cleaning, while the passengers sleep oblivious of the performance of these rites. Within a few minutes, when the 15ARs whistle away, the station foreman will be left alone on his dark platform. On a still night he can hear the engines for a full hour, exhausting in and out of phase, as they work up the grade to Wolwefontein.

96 A Class 16R leaves Swartkops junction for Port Elizabeth in June 1971. During 1969 these Hendrie Pacifics arrived from Natal where they had been displaced by electrification of the South Coast Line. They immediately replaced the Class 10BRs on the Uitenhage run, but were destined to last for only six years in this service, in contrast to over 30 years for the Elliot machines.

The Kowie Railway

The first 35 miles of this line, from the junction with the Midland Main Line at Alicedale to Grahamstown, were built under the first contract executed by George Pauling & Co., the civil engineering contractors who went on to build many thousands of miles of railway in Southern Africa.

The line to Grahamstown was part of the CGR and was completed in 1879. Soon afterwards the redoubtable Pauling set up the Kowie Railway Company to extend the railway another 44 miles to the new harbour under construction at Port Alfred. The extension was completed in 1884 and the new company began operations with four Hunslet 4-4-0Ts, but the harbour works were abandoned in 1898 because the Kowie estuary silted up more quickly than the dredgers could clear away the sand banks. The railway company, which had never really prospered, now found itself without its reason for existence, but held out for another 15 years. It was the Blaauwkrantz bridge disaster of 1911 which finally destroyed it. Thirty-one people were killed when a train derailed and fell into the gorge, and claims resulting from the accident crippled the company, forcing it to sell out to the Government in 1913.

97 *The State President's train*. For his visit to Grahamstown in June 1974, President Jim Fouché used the White Train, seen here drawn by two 19Ds, and passing a fine stand of *aloe ferox*. The rolling stock was first ordered by the SAR for the visit of King George VI in 1947, and it is difficult to imagine a more stately way to travel.

98 A GD has its fire cleaned at Alicedale before working the night train to Grahamstown, September 1965.

99 Class GD No. 2229 leaves Alicedale junction with the 12.25 pm mixed to Port Alfred, September 1965. At the rear of the train is another GD, No. 2233, which will push her up the 27-mile bank to Cold Spring, 1 500 feet higher, and the summit of the line at 2 415 feet.

Sydenham scenes

100 This early morning scene at the south end of the shed was shot in the mid-sixties, when Sydenham had an allocation of over 100 engines.

101 The shed at Sydenham, Port Elizabeth, was at one time blessed with an assortment of classes unsurpassed in South Africa. As late as 1968 one could find over 100 engines in 18 classes and nine wheel arrangements stabled here on a quiet Sunday night. In 1978 the number of classes has been reduced to six but Sydenham is still an interesting shed, particularly in the late afternoon when the 15ARs are being prepared for the evening commuter trains. This typical view of the east end of the shed shows twelve engines of 11 classes and seven different wheel arrangements in May 1962. From the left are 12AR (4-8-2), GD (2-6-2+ 2-6-2), 7(4-8-0), S2(0-8-0), 8(4-8-0), 19D(4-8-2), 12AR, 6(4-6-0), 10BR (4-6-2), 19B(4-8-2), 11(2-8-2) and 10(4-6-2).

102 The graceful profile of P.A. Hyde's Class 10 illuminated in Sydenham shed one night in September 1965.

Midland Main Line

Almost a decade has passed since the main line was converted to diesel. This was the last of the Class 1 main lines from the ports to lose steam – in 1969, just six years short of its centenary.

After main-line operation from Algoa Bay began in 1875, various early CGR locomotives were used, settling down in the 1890's to Classes 6 and 7. From 1902 Beatty's Class 8 added muscle to the Midland stud, while during the twenties Hendrie's 12B and (later) 12A became the anchor power below Cradock, with 15Bs northwards to Noupoort and De Aar. This was the position for over 30 years until the first 15Fs released by the electrification of the Cape Main Line arrived in 1957. The 15Fs enjoyed a virtual monopoly with occasional assistance from Classes 12R, 12AR and 15BR and later, diesels of Class 32, until steam was ousted from the Midland Main Line by Class 33 diesels in 1969.

103 104

103 Snow lies ahead for this 15F pounding upgrade to Sherborne on a below-freezing morning in July 1968. The four-star motif of Cradock motive power depot adorns her smokebox and she has a cowled chimney for working the long tunnels of the Midland Main Line.

104 After the 15Fs arrived at Sydenham, there was a period when they took over almost the entire service on the Midland Main Line, but by the early sixties traffic was growing to such an extent that the 12Rs were again venturing onto the high rails, at least as far as Cookhouse. The combination of 12R + 15F became increasingly common: this one is seen crossing the Bushmans River in May 1968.
The train is on a deviation opened in 1934. The original location between Paterson and Alicedale was via the notorious Bellevue bank which managed to avoid tunnels and major bridges, but was beset by severe grades and curvature which necessitated banking of both north- and southbound trains.

106

107

105 Spanning the Van Stadens River is the highest 2'-gauge railway bridge in the world, a spindly structure more than 250 feet above the water. An NGG 13 with limestone from Loerie makes its way to the Eastern Province Cement Company's exchange sidings at Chelsea.

106 A line-up of NG 15s in Humewood Road shed at night.

107 The first ever 'Apple Express' near Humewood Road in 1965. Scheduled passenger trains into the Longkloof were discontinued over 30 years ago, but until very recently it was still possible to buy a ticket for Avontuur at Humewood Road and ride the little train throughout. The journey took two full days with an overnight stop at Humansdorp but there was never a dull moment. 13 years ago the SAR began offering special day-excursions to Loerie and back. The fine scenery near the Van Stadens River Bridge and the descent and ascent of the Loerie bank are highlights of the day. These steam-hauled excursions have become increasingly popular, and during the 1977/78 summer holiday season were introduced for the first time on a regular once-weekly basis, leaving Humewood Road at 9.00 am on Saturdays.

108 A confrontation between a Kalahari and a double-decker bus at the Cape Road crossing near Chelsea in 1965. The engine was repaired and soon at work again.

Narrow narrow gauge

A fully-fledged commercially viable railway with only 24 inches between the rails seems an anachronism in 1978, yet the SAR today operates 440 miles of this ultra-narrow gauge. 178 miles belong to the Avontuur railway which runs westward into the Longkloof from Port Elizabeth, with a 17-mile branch from Gamtoos to Patensie.

The staple traffic on the lower section is limestone, moved in daily block-loads from Loerie to Chelsea. A steam locomotive of the Eastern Province Cement Company used to take over for the 12-mile haul from Chelsea over the Company's tracks down to the cement works at New Brighton. Today a diesel works this private branch.

The main reason for the existence of these lines is, however, agricultural: the products of the Longkloof provide year-round revenue, which rises to a peak during the fruit season when as many as 20 trains a day run westwards from Assegaaibos. Every year one and a half million cases of fruit for export are transported down to the pre-cooling sheds in the harbour at Algoa Bay.

The complete story of this little railway has been beautifully told in *Twenty-four Inches Apart*, by Sydney M. Moir. The first trains ran in 1903 with shapely Manning Wardle 2-6-4 Ts providing the power. These were supplemented over the years by Bagnall and Baldwin 4-6-0s, the legendary Lawley 4-4-0s from the Beira railway, and Baldwin Pacifics (Class 60).

In 1920 an event occurred on the Avontuur line which was to have a profound effect on locomotive development in South Africa. This was the arrival of the first Garratt, No. NG51, heralding an era of new Garratt construction for the SAR which would last an incredible 48 years. Garratts were used throughout the Longkloof right up to 1973. They transformed the working of the 2' gauge and certainly prolonged the usefulness of the lines. The Hanomag-built NGG13s, introduced in 1928, and the later NGG16s were able to take rough handling and yet survive on minimal maintenance.

This brings to mind a footplate ride several years ago on an NGG13 which was working a 215-ton limestone train from Loerie to the Eastern Province Cement Company's exchange sidings at Chelsea. In the regulator quadrant, a wad of cotton waste was jammed tight against the full open stop. The driving technique was hardly that laid down in the handbook: cut-off set without alteration at 55%, with the regulator either hard up against the cotton waste or closed like a tap. Rather tentatively, we asked the driver whether he ever tried a bit of expansive working, but he was adamant: 'Man', he said, 'with the fitters we've got these days, if I tried any fancy 15% cut-off, ten to one I'd have the front unit going backwards and the back unit going forwards.'

After the widening of the South West African 2'-gauge lines during 1959/60, there was a massive transfer of the more modern rolling stock. The Avontuur line benefited from the acquisition of Class NG15 2-8-2s and some brand new NGG16 Garratts from the Tsumeb Corporation, a copper-mining concern which ran its own railway and owned several locomotives.

The 2-8-2s soon became popular with the Avontuur-line crews, who nicknamed them 'Kalaharis', a not strictly correct reference to their geographical origin.

In 1973, 20 narrow-gauge diesels of Class 91 were delivered at Humewood Road, and this depot's NGG13s were all retired after 45 years of impeccable service. The NGG16s were all transferred to Natal, leaving the Avontuur line Garratt-less. Today only the Kalaharis maintain the 70-year tradition of steam into the Longkloof.

Into the Longkloof

109 The last lap for an NGG 13 between Siesta and Avontuur in July 1973.

110 You can't do this on a diesel! Joubertina, April 1976.

111 Deep in the Longkloof the mist has begun to lift from the apple orchards as this NG 15 No. 147 approaches Heights with an early-morning block of empties for the packing sheds at Louterwater in April 1977.

112 Bound for the pre-cooling sheds at Port Elizabeth harbour, a pair of Kalaharis wind cautiously down the hill from Heights with a load of export fruit in May 1974.

111

112

113 'A really useful engine' as the Rev. Awdry's Fat Controller would have put it. With their 51" drivers and 47 000-lb tractive effort, the 12ARs were ideal for the continuous 1 in 50 grades up from the coast. Heading for Queenstown is No. 1530 on the Eastern Cape's crack train, No. 434, four miles out of East London, January 1960. The nameboard commemorates the centenary of the opening of the first public railway in South Africa from Durban to Point.

114 A Class 12AR on Train 434, the East London-Johannesburg express, hammers up the 1 in 50 towards the summit tunnel at Gaika, near Cathcart, Easter 1958.

115 At East London the 1 in 40 begins right off the platform-ends. 4-up is shown leaving East London in May 1932 with Class 3B No. 1480. For us this is one of the most evocative pictures ever taken on the SAR. It shows the standard SAR passenger formation of the twenties: Hendrie engine and rake of imperial brown open-balcony clerestory coaches.

Note the engine's commodious four-window cab, a specification of her designer who came to this country from the Highland Railway where the severity of the weather made crew comfort essential. The earliest locomotives of the Eastern system had open-sided cabs as it was thought that if drivers were too comfortable they were liable to fall asleep on duty. The first winter of railroading over the Stormberg rectified that.

5 The Eastern Cape

Anyone accusing the Cape Eastern system of going round in circles before 1949 would have been right. The Eastern Main Line draped itself like spaghetti over the ridges of the Winterberg and Stormberg ranges, in order to gain height without excessive expenditure on earthworks.

At Union in 1910, the Cape Province contributed three systems to the newly-formed South African Railways and Harbours: the Eastern, the Midland and the Western systems. The first had by far the toughest operating conditions as is evident from some statistics in a paper presented in 1884 to the Institution of Civil Engineers by W. G. Brounger, one of South Africa's most famous railway civil engineers and for many years Chief Engineer of the Cape Government Railways. He reported that 21% of the Eastern lines were laid to gradients of 1 in 50 or steeper, as against 14% and 6% for the Midland and Western systems. The Eastern had 11 miles of curves of six chains or sharper radius (the minimum was five chains, equal to 330 feet), as against none on the Midland and only three on the Western. At that time the total route mileages open were 292, 589 and 643 respectively.

Between 1936 and 1949 a wholesale relocation of the railway between East London and Queenstown was undertaken by the Chief Civil Engineer's department. When the work was completed the rail distance between the two towns had been reduced by 17 miles, the ruling grade from 1 in 40 uncompensated to 1 in 50 compensated, and the curvature by an amazing 14 700 degrees, equivalent to almost 41 complete circles!

Small wonder then that the first articulated locomotives in Southern Africa were imported by the CGR for use on the main line inland from East London. These 0-6-6-0T double Fairlies, supplied by the Yorkshire Engine Company in 1875, were only moderately successful, having been designed in Britain (as were all the CGR's locomotives up to that time) to run on Welsh steam coal. The cost of shipping fuel more than 6 000 miles was prohibitive even in those days, and it became necessary to use coal from the new mines at Indwe and Molteno. The local product with its high ash content and bad clinkering was decidedly inferior. In fact, it took twice as much of the local coal to move tonnage as far as the Welsh coal, but it still worked out cheaper.

The full story of the experiment with Cape coal and its effect on future locomotive development can be found in D. F. Holland's definitive *Steam Locomotives of the South African Railways*. The problems with colonial coal limited the usefulness not only of the Fairlie engines but also of the other imported designs of the period. Some significant experiments were conducted by J. D. Tilney, first Locomotive Superintendent of the Eastern system, which led to the development of the first locomotive classes able to handle the local coal successfully. These were the old Cape Classes 3 and 5, designed in detail at Salt River under the direction of H. M. Beatty's predecessor, Michael Stephens. They had increased heating surfaces and water spaces around the firebox and much larger grates, and in old Cape Class 5 extended smokeboxes were introduced for the first time. These features

115

eventually came to be incorporated in all South African designs, even after the discovery of good quality coal on the Highveld and in Natal.

In spite of the Fairlies' greater nominal tractive effort, conventional engines proved to be more suitable for Cape Eastern conditions. In particular, Class 7 (from 1892) and Class 8 (from 1902) established themselves. In 1903 another experimental articulated type arrived at East London, the 'Kitson-Meyer' which had 0-6-6-0 wheel arrangement. But it lasted only five years, and was not a success as its boiler could not provide sufficient steam for the long continuous grades of the Eastern Main Line.

The next articulated types to be tried were Class MF simple Mallets, which were used for a few years in the twenties. For the next 30 years, non-articulated engines ruled the main line, ranging through Classes 3B, 14C, 14CR, 12AR, 15A and 15AR. Even after the opening of the newly located line to Queenstown in 1949, double-heading was common, and to eliminate it the new

GMAMs were introduced in this service in 1956. Four types of articulateds were used on the Cape Eastern system from 1875, and the GMAMs or 'Gammats' were the only really successful ones, although severely hampered by their coal capacity of only 14 tons. When they were working up the continuous 88-mile grade from East London to Gaika, re-coaling was often necessary at Amabele, only 45 miles out. This could have been avoided at the design stage if a higher axle-load had been adopted. The GMAMs, with an axle-load of only 16 tons, have spent most of their lives on routes where 21 tons is permitted. They were worked flat out up the Cape Eastern Main Line and were able to haul 900 tons up the sustained 1 in 50 banks at a constant speed of 11 mph. This was certainly one of their most impressive areas of operation until they were displaced by diesels during 1965/66.

Today the only steam remaining around East London is used for shunting and trip-working. These duties are handled by Classes 14CR and 15AR.

East London Workings

116 A 14CR on a Kingwilliamstown-East London local draws past the fine home signal at Blaney junction.

117 A Class 14CRM and 12AR double-head the daily petroleum train to the east bank industrial sites, high above Buffalo Harbour in 1977.

118 A line-up of 15ARs and 14CRs in East London shed at night.

Into the Stormberg

The Cape Eastern Main Line has been dieselised since 1966, but there are still – in 1978 – two important steam sheds along its route. The main one at Queenstown provides motive power for several sub-depots serving the various North-eastern Cape branches. Numerous locomotives are allocated away from the main depot, and a daily steam train works along the main line to bring them in for their fortnightly washouts and minor repairs. This involves a crossing of the Stormberg range via Bushmanshoek Pass at an altitude of 5 586 feet (between Sterkstroom and Molteno) for Burgersdorp engines which are used on the Aliwal North, Barkly East and Stormberg-Rosmead lines. The Stormberg-Rosmead line, completed in 1892, is an important cross-country link for traffic between the Eastern Cape and Cape Town. At Kromhoogte it crosses the Stormberg at an altitude of 5 342 feet, and the eastbound climb to this summit from Schoombie (3 851 feet) is the outstanding feature of operation of this line. Halfway up to Kromhoogte is the small town of Steynsburg where uphill trains stop for water.

Here we witnessed one night an astonishing build-up of the fire of Class 15AR No. 1818. She was the beautifully polished front engine of the double-headed, 18-coach Cape Town-East London mail.

Although it was now only 12 miles (and 600 feet of vertical climb) to the summit, the crew seemed intent on filling the firebox with the brick-sized lumps of coal in the tender. Over 300 shovelsful went onto the 37 square-foot grate before they were content to wash up and sit down. There was no sign of flame in the firebox, not even a glow, and the coal was right up to the underside of the brick arch, mounding back to the almost-blocked firebox door.

We pulled out of Steynsburg, and soon the exhaust was pulling a glow through the coals. The crew kept the firedoor open a crack to warm the cab, but at no time on the climb was the fire touched. This seemed to defy the principle of 'little and often', and at Kromhoogte our curiosity overcame us. We asked the crew how far they expected to go before putting on more coal. 'Right through to Stormberg,' was the reply. We had to leave the engine here and so could not witness this at first hand, but since then we have heard some drivers swear that they can get through from Steynsburg to Burgersdorp, a distance of 58 miles, on one fire.

119 A 19D and 15AR on the daily washout working between Queenstown and Burgersdorp, round the horseshoe curve in Bushmanshoek Pass, September 1976.

120 Working a heavy freight on the climb to Kromhoogte, this pair of 15ARs has just negotiated the horseshoe curve below Steynsburg, July 1976.

121

Cross-country Passenger

121 Class 15ARs make an impressive exit from Schoombie with the Cape Town mail in July 1976.

122 Out of a totally overcast sky a pencil sunbeam illuminates this 15AR + 19A and their Cape Town-bound mail train in 1973.

123 The double-headed 15ARs of the East London-Cape Town mail wait at Schoombie for an eastbound freight to receive orders and clear the main line in July 1975.

122

Maclear Branch

Some of the finest scenery in the Border region is to be found along this line, and to add to its attractions it is still steam-worked. Of course it was not originally built for aesthetic reasons: the Imvani-Indwe Railway Company completed the first 67 miles from Sterkstroom to Indwe with the very practical motive of tapping the coal seams there. The Company operated the line, using their own locomotives, from 1896 when it was opened until 1900 when the Cape Government took it over, presumably for strategic reasons as access to the Witbank coalfields became impossible during the Anglo-Boer War.

The way to Maclear was completed by the CGR in 1906. However, when peace returned it was no longer necessary to use the poor quality Indwe coal, and the railway began to earn its living from the fertile agricultural districts along its right of way.

Highlights in the comparatively uneventful life of this branch were the opening of the seven-mile deviation to serve the town of Dordrecht in 1932 and, more interesting, the use for over 20 years of the Class MJ and MJ1 Mallets to Maclear.

126

124 Hard frost lies thick on the ground as this 19D brings the daily (except Sundays) passenger out of Maclear, barely coping with the iced rails. The hanging clouds of condensed exhaust emphasise the fact that it can get very cold along this line which runs beneath the southern Drakensberg for most of its length. In the early 1900s a 6th Class and its train were snowbound for several days near Clarks siding, highest point on the line.

125 Late in the afternoon a domeless 19D climbs from Glenwallace to Halseton with the Maclear-Sterkstroom passenger train.

126 The Sterkstroom-Maclear train with a 19D in charge crosses the Tsolo River Bridge at Xalanga, May 1976.

Eight Reverses to Barkly East

During World War I a ship loaded with bridge material en route to South Africa was sunk by a U-boat, a disaster that was to have a profound effect on a very interesting branch line.

Earthworks were commenced between Aliwal North and Barkly East in 1902, and the rails reached Melk, the first reversing station, in 1911. To speed construction further ahead, a series of six reverses was built to take the line from Melk down to the Karringmelkspruit and up the other side to Motkop. In the meantime, a well-graded formation was prepared from the buffer-stop end of Melk reversing station to the edge of the chasm overlooking the river, over 300 feet below. A tunnel was bored through solid sandstone cliffs on the opposite bank and its far portal opened out at the buffer stop of sixth reverse.

The bridge which was intended to eliminate all these reverses would have been the highest in South Africa. The setting would have been spectacular, but somehow it is hard to beat the excitement of see-sawing through those six reverses, descending and ascending through 600 feet.

Further on, the highest altitude on any railway in the Cape Province is reached at Drizzly (6 528 feet), before the line descends via seventh and eighth reverses to the crossing of the Kraai River at Tierkrans. From here, an uphill slog through 500 vertical feet brings trains into the terminus at Barkly East.

For nearly 40 years this line was the preserve of the GBs which came here after a few years' service on the Natal South Coast. They were the first of a long line of 3' 6"-gauge branch-line Garratts used in South Africa. The very first, No. 2166 (Beyer Peacock, 1921), is preserved at Aliwal North station.

Today the Barkly East branch provides one of the most exciting railway journeys in South Africa. Not only is its operation of great interest, but it passes through some of the most dramatic landscapes in the country. The line was dieselised in April 1978.

127 A 19D brings the daily (except Sundays) Barkly East-Aliwal North goods up to second reverse. In the background its opposite number, having just departed from fourth reverse, heads out of the canyon of the Karringmelkspruit up to fifth and sixth reverses.

128 The sandstone amphitheatre surrounding sixth reverse is pierced by the unused tunnel ahead of 19D No. 2725, poised here at the buffer stop preparatory to backing down to fifth reverse in July 1977. At the other end of the short bore is a sheer drop of 300 feet to the river. The neatly dressed sandstone portals have the date of completion, 1911, carved into their keystones.

129 In her last year of service GB No. 2161 is shown watering at Lady Grey in April 1966.

130 The numberplate of the very first 3' 6"-gauge Garratt in South Africa. For over 40 years her home was the Barkly East branch, and she is now preserved at Aliwal North.

131 Backing her train up from fifth to sixth reverse is No. 2164 in June 1965. Although she must have completed this manoeuvre many thousands of times, this is one of the few photographs we know of a GB at this spectacular location.

133

132 No. 2725 was the regular engine of driver Botha and fireman Botha of Barkly East. She looked a picture as she worked out of the Kraai River Valley in June 1977.

133 A 19D on her way between Lynndale and New England in the winter of 1976. At this altitude the streamlets off the rising ground behind the train remain frozen from May to October.

134 Crossing the trout-laden Kraai River at Tierkrans, 19D No. 2744 opens out for the climb to eighth reverse, June 1975.

134

The Great Kei River Pass

For many years the SAR timetable has given the incorrect altitude for Sihota – it is actually in a depression only 558 feet above sea-level and not 1 553 feet as shown. It is situated on the right bank of the Kei, and on either side over half a mile of altitude has to be regained by trains making their exit from the gorge carved by this great river. The names of the halts on the way out – Spiral, Zigzag, Eagle – indicate the nature of the terrain for, unlike most other mountain lines, the Kei River Pass is a down-and-up affair.

The pass forms the greatest but not the only barrier on the SAR's main line into Transkei. Along routes which parallel the coast, there is always one more river to cross and the Umtata line is no exception. After the heady drop into the canyon of the Kei, the train still has to make the almost equally severe crossing of the Bashee River.

As on the Maclear branch, the ruggedness of this route warranted the use of Mallet locomotives, and the MJ and MJ1 plied these rails for almost three decades. When the last Mallets faded from service in the late fifties, the Class 14CRB bore the brunt of the work, with assistance from 19As and 19Ds. Towards the end of steam the GOs, displaced by dieselisation of the Steelpoort line, came down from the Transvaal, but they were not really given a fair trial. For a few months there was a half-hearted attempt to run the service with the GOs; then they were sent away to Natal and the diesels moved in early in 1973.

135 Mallets worked the Great Kei River Pass for many years. Here is MJ No. 1674 in her last days at East London shed in January 1961.

136 Double-headed 14CRBs bring the day train from Umtata across the Kei River at Sihota in May 1972.

137 The same train coming out of the Kei River Gorge, about two miles above the spiral.

137

138 Two 14CRBs head for Butterworth, Transkei, with a heavy goods train in December 1970.

139 *A big brew-up at Sihota*. These 14CRBs have had their fires cleaned, their rods greased and their tenders filled with Kei water, and with full heads of steam they're ready for the two hours of climbing to Komga at the uppermost rim of the gorge. May 1971.

138 139

6 The Free State Main Line

Behemoths of Bloemfontein

Dick 'Low water' Marsh backs his spotless 23, No. 3210, down the loco spur onto the front coach of Train 433. The two Class 5E electric units which brought the train into Kroonstad have handed over 25 minutes late. The guard, after waiting restlessly while the coupling is completed, hands a copy of the train-list to the driver. 'Seventeen saloons for 730 tons,' he says and stalks off to his van to wave the green flag. He waves and waves but something is wrong. Marsh is busy with monkey wrench and 4-lb hammer on the 23's turbo-generator. Another 15 minutes go by before the running repairs are completed and 433 is under way, now 40 minutes late.

As we lurch around the curves at Gunhill, Marsh puts his foot on the backhead, yanks the regulator full open, and 3210 roars exuberantly into Bosrand bank. We take 11 minutes to climb this notorious seven-mile stretch of 1 in 90, speed dropping to 30 mph, but once over the top the driver keeps her wide open. The

beautifully-tuned engine sounds like a three-cylinder machine as we race on up the easier grade to Geneva.

Less than three hours later we are standing at the home signal for Bloemfontein with five minutes to go for a right-time arrival. A few sharp whistles for South Cabin and the green eye winks us on past the wheel-tappers into platform 3, dead on time.

Marsh, at that time the senior driver at Kroonstad, could always coax a couple of hundred more horsepower out of his engine than the average engineman. He earned his nickname 'Low water' through his habit of running with the water near the

140 Train 438 is running late and Class 23 No. 3269 is making time, a mile north of Bloemfontein station in August 1971.

141 No. 438, the Johannesburg express, with a 15F in charge, gets out of Bloemfontein in winter 1967.

bottom nut of the gauge glass. In fact it is better to run with too little water in the boiler, rather than too much – short of collapsing the crownsheet, more damage is done through priming than through dropping a lead plug. However, most drivers nowadays don't put this into practice.

As the sixties ticked over into 1970, the daily struggle to clear traffic on the main lines of the Free State reached unwieldy proportions. The three main sheds, Bloemfontein, Kroonstad and Bethlehem, were allocated 179, 130 and 104 locomotives respectively, with not a diesel or 'draadkar' among them and, although the run-down of steam traction had not yet started, it was an appalling scramble to find staff to work the 'dirty' machines. During March 1969 the use of diesels on block-loads on the Kroonstad and Burgersdorp mains suddenly stopped, and for nearly two years Bloemfontein enjoyed an Indian summer of steam. An average of more than 300 train arrivals and departures took place in Bloemfontein each 24 hours – all behind steam.

Six through routes are served by Bloemfontein's marshalling yards: Kroonstad (for the Witwatersrand), Bethlehem (for Natal), Aliwal North (for Burgersdorp), Burgersdorp (for the Eastern Cape), Noupoort (for the Cape Midlands and Mossel Bay) and Kimberley (for the Western Cape). In addition, the Maseru branch off the Bethlehem line serves Lesotho. The Kroonstad line is the busiest, and during the last year of full steam operation an average of 100 trains moved over 100 000 tons per day over this route. The record gross tonnage moved by steam in one 24-hour period was 138 000 tons – remarkable for a line which is inclined at 1 in 100 for a considerable part of its length.

The end came in three stages. First to go were the Burgersdorp turns when East London diesels began to work through to Bloemfontein early in 1971. There was a period of mixed working for about a year, but by early 1972 Bloemfontein engines no longer locked couplers with their colleagues at Burgersdorp shed. During that year Midland diesels started to infiltrate the Noupoort line, which succumbed totally on 31 March 1973. Of the main lines, only the Kroonstad turns were still steam-operated.

For another three glorious years the Kroonstad route continued under billowing exhausts, but in December 1975 the catenary into Bloemfontein yards was energised and most freight workings went electric. When the station tracks were energised in March 1976, 85 years of main-line steam operations in the Orange Free State came to an end.

143

142 *Triple meet in* Steamtown. In 1970 Bloemfontein was still a 100% steam city where it was possible to see 16 different classes of locomotive in six wheel arrangements. With 300 arrivals and departures every 24 hours, scenes like this occurred almost daily at any of the five rail-over-rail flyovers in the Bloemfontein complex. Coming under the flyover is 15F No. 3136 on Train 71, the Durban mail; overhead is 16E No. 859 (at that time named 'Bloemfontein') blasting up the freight by-pass with Train 993, the Springfontein pick-up; and in the foreground is 16DA No. 873 with a local freight for the brickworks at Shannon. May 1970.

143 Awaiting the 'right away' at 9.45 pm, ex-works Class 16E No. 858 'Allan G. Watson' is about to take the 17-coach Port Elizabeth express, Train 435, down to Noupoort in September 1970. Within six months she was relegated to local freight working and was retired in June 1972, having completed only 13 000 miles since her last heavy repair. Fortunately this engine escaped the scrapper's torch. She was sent to De Aar and after five years of open-air storage was able to perform with startling efficiency on the Rhodesian Express (once), the Drakensberg Express (twice) and several goods trains, in preparation for her memorable haulage of the Union Limited and the Union Express in September 1977 (see pages 6 and 7).

142

145

146

144 *Sunrise at the shed.* 1969/70 was the peak period at Bloemfontein, when one of the SAR's greatest engine terminals was accepting or despatching engines every five minutes around the clock. All shed roads were lined three-deep with engines awaiting assignment, and not a diesel disturbed the scene.

145 Class 23 No. 3257 brings the first eastbound Drakensberg Express into platform 2 in January 1975.

146 On a Sunday in June 1969, Class 16E No. 857 – then named both 'Anne Smith' (cab sides) and 'Vereeniging' (smoke deflectors) – departs with the 8.20 am to East London, and Class 15E No. 2879 leaves with the 8.20 am to Bethlehem. In those days there were several simultaneous departures each week.

147 Double-headed 15Fs on a 2 160-ton southbound coal drag in the cutting at Van Tonder, March 1971.

148 The little dam on the Renosterspruit at Glen had its wall raised during 1972, making reflection shots like this possible. A 15F on a southbound freight in July 1973.

149 A 15F pilots a 23 on an up-goods at Karee Koppie. For the first six years of the seventies, a daily tally of 100 steam trains paraded past this natural grandstand alongside the eight-mile Glen-Karee bank. The visitors' book at Karee station was filled with the names of enthusiasts who made the pilgrimage to this spot. The last entries appeared the day before the line was finally handed over to electric traction in March 1976.

152
153

Bloemfontein South

152 As a memorable farewell to two great locomotives and a great steam main line, Class 16DA No. 872 and 16E No. 857 were run to Noupoort and back during the last week of steam on the line. The Pacifics are shown here on the return working, heading through the new Agtertang station at sunset in March 1973.

153 A running meet in CTC territory. 23s pass at Bekkersfontein in the winter of 1972.

154 The wide-firebox 16DAs were a Watson variation of the original Baldwin design. In six of these engines ordered from Henschel in 1930, he increased the grate area from 45 to 60 square feet. The modification was a success: the larger grate produced a proportionately slower rate of combustion for the same amount of work, thus causing less clinker. From that time all heavy main-line power was designed with large grates. Here is No. 874 leaving Bloemfontein on the south goods avoiding line on a misty morning in 1971.

155 In its heyday, which lasted until 1970, the South Main Line was host to a wide variety of classes, with 23s predominating. Engines on transfer – like this pair of 11s on their delivery run to South Witbank Colliery in 1973 – added to the interesting assortment.

156 A Class 23 crosses the Kaalspruit on the 5.10 pm stopper to Springfontein.

157 A 15F about to depart with the night train to Kroonstad, September 1965.

158 At the other end of the line, Class 16DAs Nos. 871 and 872 are ready to take the 1.10 am empty-stock working from Bloemfontein to Thaba Nchu in December 1972.

7 Free State Trunk Routes

East to Bethlehem

As the crossroads of the Republic, the Orange Free State has the highest proportion of through, or trunk, routes of any system. Some could certainly be called main lines in their own right, and the grouping of lines in Chapters 6 and 7 is arbitrary.

The two most interesting trunk routes are Bloemfontein-Modderpoort-Bethlehem, for its mountain scenery, and Bloemfontein-Kimberley for its heavy traffic: and the two enjoy the spotlight in these pages.

In terms of motive power they have been treated on an equal footing with the main line for almost 50 years and, indeed, the Kimberley line has for many years been operated largely by Classes 25 and 25NC, a luxury denied the main line. Although it has declined in importance since the Kroonstad-Bethlehem electrification, the Modderpoort route has also used 25NCs since 1974, and Bethlehem is the only Free State shed to stable these machines.

159 One that didn't make it: a 25 NC has her fire cleaned at Fouriesburg in April 1976. In fact, the 25 NCs are remarkably free steamers.

160 No. 872 works the Saturdays-only 2.00 pm Bloemfontein-Modderpoort up to Waghorn in September 1971, with the Thaba Nchu mountain in the background.

161 Mechanical stoker controls.

162 Driver Joubert is extremely proud of the brasswork on his 3415.

163 Here Class 25NCs double-head the Saturdays-only Ficksburg-Johannesburg train near Ionia.

Special Movements

164/165 Re-enacting scenes typical of 30 years earlier, Class 6J No. 641 and Class 8 No. 1104 struggle out of Bethlehem with a freight for Frankfort in September 1969.

166 A Class 12R and 15F work up the 1 in 50 out of Bethlehem on the Saturdays-only passenger to Ficksburg in December 1973. This train was regularly double-headed at long weekends when extra coaches were attached to cater for mineworkers returning to Lesotho.

167 For the benefit of RSSA members who had hired coaches on the train, No. 71-down was double-headed with narrow- and wide-firebox 16DAs in November 1972. Here the train is leaving Generaalsnek, drawn by Nos. 848 and 876.

164

The main lines from the Western, Midland and Eastern Cape systems had all reached the Vaal River by 1892, forming a recognisable pattern focusing on the goldfields of the Witwatersrand. The remainder of the Orange Free State railway map filled in slowly, the newest link in the trunk-line network, from Allanridge to Ancona, being completed only in 1967.

The Cape Government had financed the building of the main line because the CGR stood to benefit most from it. The CGR also provided all the rolling stock and motive power, including some of its best engines, the 6th Class, for passenger work. Then on 1 January 1897 the Free State Republic took over all railways within its borders, and R. E. Brounger, son of the CGR's Chief Engineer, was appointed Director General. The new Orange Free State Railways decided to purchase locomotives of its own, choosing only Class 6 engines, with slight modifications such as larger cabs.

The Anglo-Boer War stopped construction of new lines and deliveries of new locomotives for a time, but within six years of the Treaty of Vereeniging in 1902 the main trunk railways had been completed, and the Free State had established itself as the bridge between Natal and Cape, and Transvaal and Cape networks.

All motive power was of Classes 6, 7 and 8, and double-heading on the mountainous Bloemfontein-Bethlehem route was common. Re-laying with heavy rail began in the twenties, and by the early thirties allowed the heaviest main-line power on all the main trunk lines.

The Free State system is characterised by a number of secondary through lines and branches whose main function is to clear the heavy seasonal grain traffic. The re-laying programme has been extended to these in recent years and today over 60% of the Free State network can carry the heaviest main-line locomotives.

Bloemfontein West:
Climbing to Kloofeind

168 In May 1973, driver Barnard brings his dazzling 3286 past Alex junction near Beaconsfield, with the White Train conveying State President Jim Fouché to his official residence in Bloemfontein.

169 The last passenger run of No. 857 was in December 1972, when she performed like a teenager on Trains 92 and 93 between Bloemfontein and Kimberley. The load was increased to 11 bogies consisting of twin diner and baggage van – and eight coaches crammed with enthusiasts.

170 The driver and guard of the westbound Orange Express five minutes before departure time at platform 2, Bloemfontein.

171

172

138

171 The eastbound Drakensberg Express passes a freight headed by a Class 25NC at Kloofeind. After a period when it ran only between Johannesburg and Durban, the Drakensberg was inaugurated on the Cape Town-Durban route in January 1975. The train utilises the air-conditioned stock of the old Blue Train. It has provision for the cars of passengers in specially-adapted goods wagons behind the baggage van – hence its nickname, 'the green mixed'. Between Bloemfontein and De Aar the Drakensberg was almost certainly the classiest steam train in the world in 1978.

172 Ex-works, a Class 24 and a 12AR receive some attention at Kloofeind on a run-in-turn cum delivery run to Beaconsfield shed.

173 This beautifully executed brass eagle belonged originally to driver Calitz of 25NC No. 3413. After moving from engine to engine, it now adorns Class 12A No. 1547, 'Stephanie', at De Aar shed.

174 Train 222 carrying manganese ore from Postmasburg to Newcastle, works hard on the eastbound climb up to Kloofeind behind a 25NC and a rebuilt 25 in April 1977.

174

8 Natal, the Garratt Province

The Eternal Hills

For centuries the face of Natal has been etched by the paths of animal migrations and human wanderings. In winter the parched yellow landscape has a sombre quality but in summer the hills are green and vivid. It was Portuguese explorers in search of a sea-route to the East who gave Natal its name. When Vasco da Gama and his men sighted land on Christmas Day 1497, they called it 'Natal' (birth) in honour of the day. If they had discovered this green coast on some other day of the year, they might well have named it 'Formosa' (beautiful).

The railway builders who arrived in the second half of the 19th century made their way along the most obvious routes through the hills, following the curve of the landscape. There were many times when a single bridge or tunnel would have saved miles of twisting, climbing and descending, but they lacked the capital and the sophisticated machinery to take short cuts and the line went the long way round. Over the years much of the Natal Main Line was re-located to improve the original alignment, but the branches from Pietermaritzburg have retained their earlier character. Steam operation on these lines was as spectacular and exciting as any the world has seen.

175 The first locomotives that set out to conquer these hills were ludicrously small tank engines, but the larger engines that followed were more of a match for the terrain. The Garratts made Natal their own, and in later years it could truly be called the Garratt Province. As late as 1968, Garratts accounted for 61% of the non-electric road mileage, with 223 of SAR's 393 Garratts assigned to the Natal system. But by 1974, when this photograph was taken of an eastbound train climbing towards Donnybrook, far-reaching changes were taking place which within a short space of time would eliminate these Garratts and bring to an end some 100 years of 3′ 6″ steam on the hills of Natal.

The Greytown Line

It is 2.30 am on a still clear African night. The winter landscape is cold and grey in the moonlight. Out of the east comes the distant whistle of an approaching train, and in a few minutes another sound comes drifting up the valley. At first it is muffled, then slowly it becomes more distinct – the unmistakable sound of double-headed Garratts. The rails must be wet from the dew for the distant exhausts move in and out of synchronization as the engine units, fore and aft, slip and then grip on the 1 in 30 grade. In the moonlight a trail of condensed steam lifts into the sky, occasionally reflecting a glow of orange as it tapers off behind the train. The tracks below the train are invisible but each curve is outlined by the rising steam.

Then comes a succession of violent slips as they struggle at the double 'S' half a mile down the line from us. From somewhere down the valley comes the whistle of a second train – they're running 'permissive' tonight.

More slipping and it seems the train must stall, but the second engine, back on drier track, takes hold and manages to keep them moving. Now they're out of the 'S' and on the straight. As they come into view, headlamps blazing, the exhausts of the two GMAs fill the sky. The first engine lumbers past us. The roll of two water tanks precedes the second and her piercing exhaust drowns her partner's as she comes alongside us. Then her leading unit slips wildly, and sparks fly from the wheel rims and drop from

176

176 Trains for the Greytown line are made up either at Mason's Mill or at Victoria Yard. Here, in the early morning, a GF and GMA prepare for the seven-mile, 52-curve climb from Victoria to Claridge. Most trains rated double GMAs, but the smaller Garratts used on the branches from Greytown and Schroeders were often paired with their bigger cousins when they were being brought to or from washouts. The morning pick-up, No. 1122, was the usual train for this combination and it was one of the last to go diesel, surviving until October 1974.

177 Exerting all of 137 600 lbs' tractive effort, these two GMAs heave mightily to start their train from City View siding. Within moments their flanges will sing out as they take the 'Balloon' and change direction by 180 degrees to crawl up the hillside.

the ashpan until the driver, now silhouetted in the cab, shuts the throttle. The train slows down noticeably but the front engine carries on until the one behind opens up once more and together the two giants tramp off towards the summit at Claridge, their rhythmic exhausts losing volume as the rails near us take up the sound of the rumbling wagons loaded with mine props.

As the red light on the guard's van fades in the distance, the sounds of the receding and approaching trains combine with a strange stereophonic effect. The first train reaches the summit and the second, also double-headed, grows louder. She must be past Otto's Bluff, perhaps even nearing Hardingsdale, not a mile down the track. It is now 3 am and the second train is approaching rapidly on rails less wet than before. Soon she'll be upon us and off into the night.

We all have our memories from the great days of steam, for each country had its own area of spectacular operation. America had Sherman Hill and Horseshoe Curve, England had the Lickey Incline and Shap, and Austria had Semmering. Here in South Africa we had our showplaces too, and the Greytown Line was one of the most celebrated.

During one 24-hour period there were 11 scheduled freight departures east from Pietermaritzburg – no less than seven double-headed. Trains would leave Victoria Yard and immediately attack the steep grades through Mountain Rise and Belfort to City View, where the whole of Pietermaritzburg spreads out in the valley below. Crossings were often made here, and the sight of trains restarting and immediately entering the 'Balloon', a 300-foot radius horseshoe on a 1 in 30 uncompensated grade (equivalent to 1 in 24), was unforgettable. Another mile of maximum grade including a double-horseshoe brought the train to the summit at Claridge from where it was downgrade all the way to Albert Falls. Beyond to Greytown there was hardly a mile of level track – the entire line was a succession of 1 in 30s, up and down.

But the real show was on the westbound climb from Albert Falls to Claridge, where trains were always fully loaded. The sound of two locomotives with eight cylinders converting steam power to reciprocating motion, driving four sets of 8-coupled wheels, was monumental. But after a decade of regular Garratt double-heading the diesels moved in during August 1974. By the end of the year, Mason's Mill Shed looked like a graveyard, with most of its 102 Garratts lying out of use. Today it is home for a few steam shunters (also due to be replaced shortly) and just 12 Garratts, 10 of them 2'-gauge and sub-shedded at Estcourt and Mid-Illovo. The two remaining GMAs are normally used for shunting, but they have gone out on the line recently to front passenger excursions – pleasant enough but surely no substitute for the days when Pietermaritzburg was the Garratt capital of South Africa.

178 Real action! Mechanical stokers are feeding coal as fast as it will go into the fireboxes of these two GMAs climbing between City View and Claridge, but judging from the black smoke, most of the coal is leaving the chimneys unburnt.

179 180

179 Most difficult climb for Garratts on the Greytown branch was the nine-mile ascent between Albert Falls and Claridge. Fully-loaded trains, having taken water at the twin columns at the Falls, found restarting no easy task on winter mornings when near-frozen journal boxes and sticking brakes prevailed. These two GMAs fill the sky with exhaust steam as they begin to move; the leading driver has the staff, the firemen are turning on their stokers, and if all goes well the train will crest the summit in 40 minutes.

180 The notorious S-curve above Hardingsdale was the anxiety of many a good driver. Even on a clear dry day if your engine was not in peak condition you had to hope for the best. This was a good day, the engines had a full head of steam, and the curve merely slowed the train down – to 10 mph.

The Cape-Natal Railway

South Africa has many lines with a reputation for operating severity, but few can compare with the Cape-Natal line which crosses three major watersheds between Pietermaritzburg and Franklin. The journey involves 7 000 feet of climbing and 4 000 feet of descending, with a grade of 1 in 40 uncompensated. In 140 miles of meandering it covers only 74 air miles.

Leaving Pietermaritzburg, the railway climbs along the Umsunduze River, and then follows a tributary to the summit at Elandskop, gaining 2 500 feet in 37 miles. After this first watershed, the line drops through side kloofs and along streams to the Umkomaas River at Deepdale, losing 1 785 feet in 22 miles. Over the river, the line climbs into another cross valley and up to Sizanenjana. From here it twists and turns up the slopes of the valley to a neck which commands a beautiful view back down towards the Umkomaas. From Inglenook the line encounters easier country over the last five miles into Donnybrook. It has climbed 1 682 feet in the 21 miles from Deepdale to Donnybrook.

181 Seventeen miles and nearly 1 000 vertical feet up the valley from Pietermaritzburg is Henley Halt, the first service stop for westbound trains. After helping themselves to water from the dam, these two GMAs get under way on the climb to Elandskop.

182 Trains leaving Deepdale for Pietermaritzburg cross the watershed of a tributary of the Umkomaas River. A couple of miles from Deepdale, the line climbs past an impressive waterfall on the main river whose Zulu name means cow whale – a rather descriptive name for the ungainly GMAs which operated within sight of it.

181 182

148

West of Donnybrook, the view out over the Umzimkulu ('great river' in Zulu) must rank as one of the finest in all South Africa (see pages 140-141), with the whole range of the Drakensberg blocking the horizon to the north. The railway plunges down, hugging the steep, eroded hillsides, past Zulu kraals overlooking deep krantzes, and finally reaches the Umzimkulu River at Centocow. It has lost another 1 366 feet in 20 miles. Now the final climb begins, first along the gorge of the Ingangwana River, then branching up lesser streams, and at last reaching the highest point on the line midway between Singizi and Llewellyn. The line has gained 2 300 feet in 33 miles of climbing, but the last few miles are downhill, and the altitude at Franklin is just under 5 000 feet.

Amazingly enough, the first locomotives to operate this line were small 4-8-2 tank locomotives, which the old NGR had in plenty. Until 1904 when the Hendrie B 4-8-0s (later SAR Class 1) arrived for the main line, the entire NGR fleet of 228 locomotives were tank types. Coincidentally, 1904 was also the year that the first section of the Cape-Natal railway, the 37 miles from Pieter-

maritzburg to Elandskop, was opened. Work slowed down after that. The line only reached the Cape border (near Centocow) in 1909, and the final section to Franklin was completed in 1912.

The Cape-Natal railway was originally intended to push further south and link up with the lines to Maclear and Umtata in the Transkei. Several feasible routes were surveyed, but the mountainous terrain was very difficult. Construction stopped in 1924 when the railway from Franklin reached Matatiele and Kokstad, respectively 60 and 80 miles from Maclear and Umtata as the crow flies.

The Cape-Natal railway did not become a through railway after all, but it served a well-populated area with some rich farming land and agricultural and passenger traffic soon outstripped the capacity of the small tank engines. What was needed was a large locomotive, capable of running on the light track of the time.

The solution was the Garratt, the engine which was to enjoy a 40-year monopoly until the diesels took over in 1974.

First came GCs, then GDs, GCAs and GFs, all double-six coupled types. In 1947 the GEAs, the first double-eight coupled Garratts to operate on the Cape-Natal section, were introduced. With their 51-foot-square hand-fired grates and enormous appetite for coal, they were rather unpopular with firemen. There was clearly a need for mechanically-stoked engines – a need satisfied by the introduction of GO Garratts in 1954. These were soon followed by the larger GMAs which held sway until the end of steam.

183 Showing how a Garratt articulates, a GMA storms around a tight curve near Donnybrook. The daily (except Sunday) all-stations train to Franklin, No. 1213, used to make 43 stops during its ten hours and 20 minutes of travelling, averaging 13½ mph over the distance. Travellers in a hurry could take the night train, No. 1227, which made only 31 stops and took 9 hours and 58 minutes – an average speed of just over 14 mph! Station names range from the English Creighton and Henley, to the Zulu, such as Kwa-Guzu, Mbongweni and Songonzima, to the Afrikaans Elandskop, Plessislaer and Pietermaritzburg.

184 Old stone bridges are on the endangered list in South Africa, since re-locations and the erection of heavy-duty concrete bridges have eliminated many of them. This lovely old three-arch, dressed-stone structure stands below Sizanenjana. A GCA is shown crossing on its way to Donnybrook with a pick-up freight.

185 It's a few minutes past midnight on the morning of August 23 1973, and the first of two nightly passenger trains from Franklin has just arrived at Donnybrook. A light coating of fresh snow covers the ground as the GMA prepares to be on her way. In less than 20 minutes the next train will collect the remaining passengers, waiting impatiently on this cold night.

186 Here in 'tropical Africa', the Drakensberg is usually under snow during the South African winter (May-September), and there are also occasional snowfalls in the Natal Midlands. In August 1973 the daily (except Sunday) Pietermaritzburg – Franklin train, No. 1213, threaded its way through fresh snow at 10.20 am on the final approach to Elandskop.

187 In the gorge of the Ingangwana River, between Centocow and Riverside, the railway skirts the river's edge before crossing a two-span girder bridge. When winter turns the grass to yellow, the aloes on the hillside and those cultivated around the kraals come into full bloom, splashing the landscape with bright reds. This was the rural setting of the last regular steam turn on this line, the daily pick-up from Donnybrook to Franklin.

188 Scene at a rural station. In Africa, the umbrella also does duty as a sun-shade.

189 Dual-gauge trackage is rare in South Africa, the longest stretch being a section of three miles from Donnybrook to Donnybrook Junction. Before 1974 it was possible to see Garratts of both gauges along here, but now only 2'-gauge steam engines come into Donnybrook as the 3' 6" line is diesel-operated. Back in 1973 when Donnybrook was 100% steam this GMA brought its train from Franklin over the dual-gauge section, two miles from Donnybrook.

188

187 189

In the shadow of the Drakensberg

190 Branch line and branch-line Garratt. The Underberg branch remained steam for over a year after the Cape-Natal line was dieselised, and it was the last stamping ground of the GCA Garratts. Trains were usually mixed, but on this morning in August 1973 the freight traffic was minimal and this short train was the right length to fit a picture dominated by the snow-covered peaks of the Drakensberg.

The Drakensberg Mountains range for 700 miles from the Eastern Cape along the Lesotho and Orange Free State borders with Natal and into the Transvaal, but nowhere is the escarpment more beautiful than in the 120 miles through Natal. In this area only two SAR branches approach the mountains: one from Estcourt to Bergville, 25 miles from the escarpment, and the more southerly Donnybrook-Underberg branch which stops 20 miles short of the berg.

There is something of a Swiss atmosphere here, although unfortunately there is no rack section to the top. Nevertheless, the mountains appear to be almost on top of the viewer, rising in a seemingly impenetrable barrier over a mile high.

191 The last regularly scheduled steam train from Pietermaritzburg to Donnybrook was No. 1219 which usually left Pietermaritzburg shortly after 1 pm. It was used to return Donnybrook and Franklin locomotives to work on the branches after their bi-weekly washouts at Mason's Mill, and was regularly double-headed, the combination often GCA and GF as it is here. On this Sunday it was running late, and the engines stormed through Edendale in a great hurry.

192 *Never out of sight of the Drakensberg.* The Matatiele branch leaves Franklin by running due north and climbing steeply to Swartberg, then dropping gently into the valley of the Umzimvubu River and paralleling the mountains in a wide valley before reaching Matatiele. The track is light and so is the freight traffic, and so the line was exclusively in the hands of GFs until the arrival of diesels.

193 The Matatiele passenger train had the distinction of being the last proper passenger train pulled by GFs and until 1972 the last passenger train on the SAR with a complete set of clerestory coaches. But by the time this photograph was taken in July 1974, the intrusion of steel coaches had already marred the train's classic contours, and within a few months diesels took over.

193

West to Griqualand East

Griqualand East is the windswept mountainous area which separates the Cape Province proper from that part of it which is more closely linked with Natal. A section of it was incorporated into Transkei in 1976, but the remaining areas are still administered from Cape Town although cut off from the Cape. To end this anomaly, it is probable that the remaining areas of Griqualand East will be incorporated into Natal. If this happens, the furthermost extensions of the old Cape-Natal railway will no longer reach the Cape.

9 South Coast Narrow Gauge

The Toy Garratts

The small toy train climbs up on its narrow gauge from the Umzimkulu valley into the hills. It climbs up to Carisbrooke, and when it stops there, you may get out for a moment and look down on the great valley from which you have come. It is not likely the train will leave you, for there are few people here, and everyone will know who you are. And even if it did leave you, it would not much matter; for unless you are a cripple, or very old, you could run after it, and catch it for yourself.

If there is mist here, you will see nothing of the great valley. The mist will swirl about and below you, and the train and the people make a small world of their own. Some people do not like it, and find it cold and gloomy. But others like it, and find in it mystery and fascination, and prelude to adventure, and an intimation of the unknown. The train passes through a world of fancy, and you can look through the misty panes at green shadowy banks of grass and bracken. Here in their season grow the blue agapanthus, the wild watsonia, and the red-hot poker, and now and then it happens that one may glimpse an arum in a dell. And always

behind them the dim wall of the wattles, like ghosts in the mist.

It is interesting to wait for the train at Carisbrooke, while it climbs up out of the great valley. Those who know can tell you with each whistle where it is, at what road, what farm, what river.

Alan Paton

This passage from *Cry, the Beloved Country* captures the charm of the narrow-gauge SAR lines in Natal. Two of these – the Port Shepstone-Harding line and the Umzinto-Donnybrook line – start on the South Coast. The first, previously known as the Alfred County Railway, runs 76 miles inland and climbs to 2 885 feet. The Umzinto-Donnybrook line (formerly the Stuartstown line) is 98 miles long and reaches an altitude of 4 617 feet. Its Madonela-Ixopo branch, 17 miles long, first climbs from Ixopo (3 253 feet) to Stainton (3 720 feet), and then drops sharply into the Umzimkulu Valley, losing 1 262 feet in the last 13 miles.

These narrow-gauge lines remain 100% steam and fully Garratt-operated. They are impressive not only because they are

194

very busy by comparison with narrow-gauge lines elsewhere in the world and run through such fine scenery, but also because the world's youngest Garratt locomotives operate here. These NGG 16s, eight in all, were built in 1967-68, the last new steam locomotives purchased by the SAR. Their original design dates back to 1928, making a production period of 40 years – a good record for any locomotive type. With luck, their operation may continue into the 21st century.

194 The green hills of Natal – and one of the world's youngest Garratts. As in other parts of South Africa Garratts run in reverse here, but on both the South Coast lines they normally run inland chimney-first, returning 'backwards'.

195 A sub-tropical departure from Esperanza, as an Ixopo-bound train leaves the dual-gauge and goes on 2'-gauge at the start of the long climb inland. During the winter months this train may run into snow storms when it reaches higher ground.

196 Wattle plantations create a forest-like setting for this section of the Port Shepstone-Harding narrow gauge.

195

196

The Sugar Tramways

It's a summer morning in Natal, sunny, hot and humid, but it's cool in the shady forest up the line from Nil Desperandum. We're riding a cane train with wheels more square than round, bouncing slowly up the steep grade. Riding these small 4-wheel cane wagons is an unnerving experience, particularly when you're straddling two. Loosely coupled, they jerk violently, not only backwards and forwards, but also from side to side. We're not doing more than 10 mph but the ground between the rails whizzes past in a blur.

Holding tightly onto the hand-brake wheel, we crane our necks to see what lies ahead. The view is blocked by the six tons of cane piled high in each truck so we decide to climb on top. Loose pieces of cane fall off and there's dust everywhere, but up top there's a cooling rush of air and the view is much improved. Along the length of the train, we can see the bobbing heads of the brakemen, also riding high.

Suddenly the summit tunnel looms ahead, a 700-foot bore through solid rock, and we climb down quickly, just in time to get a secure hold before plunging into darkness. The noise, loud before, becomes deafening and it's hard to breathe in the hot smoky atmosphere. It becomes even more oppressive, then there's a hint of light ahead which quickly gets brighter – and we burst out into the open and the sweet fresh air.

With a succession of loud bangs the slack between the wagons is taken up and the train comes to a stop. Thankful to be all in one piece, we jump down and walk unsteadily towards the front of the train.

The engine has already been uncoupled and driver Govender Moonsamy has just cleared the points and is backing down the loop alongside the train. With a wave he heads off again towards the tunnel and Nil Desperandum. For him and his crew it has been just another trip: in fact, he will do two more today. For us it is an experience never to be repeated. That was February 1970, and within a week the last cane trains were to run on the Sezela tracks.

During the heyday of the Natal sugar lines some 18 systems were in operation, six of them along the South Coast. The original plantations were on the North Coast, but a number of enterprising men saw the possibility of sugar farming south of Durban, even though the land was very hilly. One of these pioneers, John Bazley, moved into the area in 1859 when it was still indigenous forest and established a 600-acre plantation which he named Nil Desperandum. Earlier in his career, he had been an assistant to George Stephenson, builder of the famous 'Rocket', and using various innovative methods he soon made a success of his isolated project. Others followed and before long the whole of the South Coast was dotted with plantations and mills.

At first the cane was brought in on ox-drawn sledges. Later narrow-gauge rails began to lace the hillsides – with oxen still providing the motive power. By the turn of the century the steam locomotive had begun to take over, but oxen were used on the light field rails until the end of the tramways.

Slowly small estates were absorbed into larger ones and whole empires were built on sugar. The Reynolds brothers eventually took over various estates including Nil Desperandum, and established a new mill at Sezela on the SAR South Coast line. In later years their empire included Umtwalumi Valley, Sezela, Beneva and Esperanza Estates, all with railways which at their peak totalled 125 route miles operated by 26 steam and 12 diesel locomotives. Further north were two other estates with steam railways. The nearer one was Renishaw which lasted until 1968. The other was Illovo which continued to run 3' 6"-gauge steam at its mill as well as a dieselised 2' line but when that closed in 1977, the era of South Coast tramways came to an end.

198

197 Maids-of-all-work on Natal's sugar tramways were the classically simple 0-4-0 tank locomotives. Of nine different wheel arrangements of locomotives supplied to the various lines, nearly 40% were of this one type. Easy on maintenance and on the track, yet powerful for their size since all weight was adhesive, they were deservedly popular. Sezela had eight and most were used in the heaviest and most arduous work right to the end. No. 6, built by Avonside in 1923, is seen here at 45 years of age, blasting out of the summit tunnel. The bufferbeam passengers who rode on the front where it was cool and usually smoke-free were kept busy sanding the rails. It was a difficult task in the gloom of the tunnel but an important one, for if their judgement was wrong or their aim bad the whole train could come slipping to a stop, with nightmarish consequences.

198 The simple chunky lines of the same mountain-climbing 0-4-0 T, No. 6, show clearly in the morning light at Nil Desperandum in October 1968.

199 200
201

199 Green is the colour of the Natal South Coast – and green was the colour of most of the sugar tramway locomotives. Illovo Sugar Estates operated two systems, a 3′ 6″ line around the mill and down to the SAR connection, and a 2′ line which extended over 20 miles inland, reaching an altitude of about 2 000 feet. Diesels virtually replaced steam on the narrow gauge in the 1950s but the 'standard gauge' continued with steam, an ex-SAR Class 4-8-2 T sharing duties with this unusual Kerr Stuart, No. 1, built in 1920.

200 To three generations of Natalians and up-country visitors alike, the South Coast meant the sea – and the sugar lines. Driving south along the main coastal road, one would see the tiny trains in the fields and ride over their level crossings. They looked like toys but were good workers – witness Esperanza's No. 2 knee-deep in the fields collecting fresh cane in September 1959.

201 Far from home, some 16 miles up the Woodcote line from Sezela Mill, an 0-4-0 T takes water at the Ifafa River. Further down the line and near the Mill, the rails cross the river from which the company takes its name – 'Sezela,' meaning 'to smell out'. The name comes from the tale of a notorious crocodile with an uncanny ability to smell out victims, which lived in this river until the great Zulu chief, Shaka, came by one day with an impi, and killed the creature.

202 The Wincanton line on Beneva Estate included reverses (switch-backs), 1 in 25 grades, and double-heading in consequence. Engines used were generally 0-4-0 Ts from Sezela. At various times on this day in October 1968 the train was single-headed, double-headed, and even banked (once), as she made her way cautiously down from Wincanton.

203 0-4-0 Ts were typical, but they were not the only engines on the sugar estates. At the opposite end of the spectrum at Sezela were two rather special locomotives – Bagnall Meyer articulated tanks. The first two were built in 1936 by Bagnall for the sugar tramways, from a design based on Meyer's original concept patented in 1861. Six were eventually built for Natal, the last two coming out of the works in 1951. Sezela acquired their two second-hand from Darnall (on the North Coast) when that system closed in 1967, and they were used during the last two seasons. Pictured is No. 13, 'Mbozama', on February 14, 1970, one week before the official closing of the railway.

204 A unique feature of the Bagnall Meyer was its circular firebox with closed ashpan. This was necessary because the rear bogie joint was directly under the firebox and the only way to clear ash was through a small opening under the firedoor.

205 An English variation of the Heisler geared engine added interest to some rosters. Five two-cylinder and two four-cylinder models were built. The four-cylinder engines operated at Illovo before giving way to diesels in the early 1960s. Last to operate was this two-cylinder model, photographed on the Renishaw Estate in 1968.

10 Along the Indian Ocean

The South Coast Line

Eighty years ago the South Coast of Natal could have been called the Coast of Railway Sleepers. Shipwrecks have been common on this coast ever since the first recorded disaster in 1552, and in the early 1900s ships with cargoes of railway sleepers from Java were lost here. They left the coastline awash with flotsam which was eventually declared a menace to shipping. It must have been frustrating for the builders of the South Coast Line – opened to Park Rynie in 1897 and to Port Shepstone in 1907 – to see sleepers lying useless on the nearby shore.

A railway parallel to and very near the coast in such a lovely setting was an incentive to development. Holiday bungalows, then hotels and finally towns sprang up along the length of the railway and today this is one of South Africa's premier resort areas. The influx of so many people endangers the character of the area, but fortunately the sub-tropical foliage camouflages the worst aspects of man's intrusion.

But one kind of visual pollution very difficult to conceal is caused by the electrification of the railway. The tall poles and high wires of 'progress' reached Kelso in 1968, and Port Shepstone in 1970. No longer do passengers view the endless beaches and thick undergrowth from behind a steam locomotive: all-steel, sliding-door electric suburban stock, complete with vinyl seats, has replaced the quaint wooden coaches with swing doors.

Locomotives used on the South Coast during the last few years of steam were 15CA and 15CB Mountains and Class 16 Pacifics on the fast trains, and small-wheeled Class 14R Mountains on the stopping trains. After the electrification to Kelso, the Pacifics were transferred to the Port Elizabeth area, and the 15CAs, which could not run beyond Kelso anyway, went to the North Coast. Only the 14Rs remained to hold the fort.

In the early days the nine major river crossings were over rickety old iron and steel structures, placed well inland. Trains had to slow down for a sharp curve inland and again for the screw-piled deckspans before continuing on their way on the opposite bank. Only the lightest engines could be used and for years these were tank engines of A and G Classes until SAR's second Garratt design, the GB, was introduced in 1921. For many years afterwards this was entirely Garratt country with GCs and GCAs as the standard power, until a bridge replacement programme started in the 1950s allowed heavier locomotives to be used.

206 The blue Indian Ocean and white sandy beaches spread out majestically behind a Durban-bound train seen crossing the Mtwalume River in June 1969. The locomotive is No. 1746, a 14R.

207 As grandmother would have seen it: a typical river-crossing in the good old days when people arrived at their holiday cottages in the horse-drawn carts which picked them up at the station. A Class A tank crosses the Umkomaas River on a Port Shepstone train, circa 1915.

206

208

209

210

170

Durban and the Natal Main Line

How a railway is to drag itself up and round all these thousand-and-one spurs running into one another, with no distinct valley or flat between, is best known to the engineers and surveyors who have declared it practicable.   Lady Barker, 1875.

The sceptics were amazed when the railway from Durban to Pietermaritzburg reached its destination in 1880, for building a line through such hilly countryside was a formidable undertaking. The first 30 miles to Botha's Hill were laid on an almost continuous grade of 1 in 30 uncompensated, with only one tunnel as the line wound up the hills, occasionally finding itself high up on the edge of some deep chasm which had to be bridged. The Inchanga was the longest (567 feet) and the highest (90 feet) of the viaducts, a spidery structure said to sway on windy days.

When the first passenger trains began running in December 1880, the scheduled time was 6 hours and 14 minutes for the 71 miles. The annual footrace between these two towns, the Comrades Marathon, has been run in 5 hours and 42 minutes – in the uphill direction – but then the road distance is only 55 miles!

The Transvaal gold rush in the 1880s spurred on railway construction, and the line pushed rapidly inland from Pietermaritzburg: up the Town Hill to Hilton Road, on to the highest point at Dell (5 035 feet), before dropping steeply to Estcourt, then on across the high undulating grasslands to Colenso, Ladysmith and Newcastle and the final upward push (via reverses) to Laing's Nek (5 399 feet) and Charlestown. Over the 304-mile distance the total vertical climb was 12 600 feet.

For thirteen years after it was completed in 1891 the entire line was operated by tank locomotives, 4-8-2Ts and 4-10-2Ts, sometimes three to a train! In 1904 the arrival of the first tender engines, the Hendrie B 4-8-0s (later SAR Class 1) revolutionised workings and from that time locomotive development was rapid. First came the Hendrie D 4-8-2s (SAR Class 3) and American Mallets for banking, in 1909-10. Then in 1914 the 'ultimate' Natal Main Line locomotive, the Class 14 'Mountain' 4-8-2, was introduced. This was to remain the resident main-line engine type, with the notable exception of the six GL Garratts and a few other experimental types, until electrification, started in 1924, was completed in 1939.

From 1916, major deviations and alternative main-line routes were introduced, making the task easier for steam and for the 'box-cabs' which followed. But the original Natal Main Line to Pietermaritzburg via Pinetown was only electrified in 1959, and by that time some of the 14s had done 45 years' hard labour on the line for which they were designed – SAR's most difficult main line.

208 The Point was home for SAR's last tank engines, the H2 4-8-2 Ts. These were converted to 8-coupled from the original Reid 4-10-2 Ts, and were used in shunting duties for many years until displaced by more modern engines. Many drifted into industrial work and until recently some were still operating in this capacity. SAR's remaining H2s were slowly reduced to ten by early 1975. Then the axe fell and by the year's end all were retired.

209 Durban's train shed was opened in 1898 and has been in continuous use ever since, but it will not last much longer. A new station is being built on the site of the old steam shed of Greyville which was closed in November 1976, ending 116 years of steam operation in Durban. In 1969 a steam special was run up the main line to mark the passing of steam passenger trains from the Durban area.

210 If the 1969 steam excursion created a precedent, the 1974 trip to Pietermaritzburg was a fitting finale to Durban's main-line steam. The two 14Rs were brilliantly clean, and the lead engine even had a polished brass dome. These 60-year-olds not only looked good – they performed impeccably.

211 The 31-mile Rossburgh-Cato Ridge deviation was opened in 1921, providing an alternative route more easily graded (1 in 66) than the old main line. Until electrification in 1936, the sounds of steam engines such as this Class 14 4-8-2 on an upgrade passenger echoed in Shongweni Gorge. The offbeat exhausts of South Africa's largest Garratts, the Class GL 4-8-2+ 2-8-4s, were heard here too from 1929.

By rail to Zululand

The road to Zululand has been shrouded in mystery and intrigue ever since the first traders tramped this way from Durban early in the 19th century. They were followed by missionaries, emissaries of colonial governments, settlers, and a host of unsavoury opportunists bent on personal gain. At this time the Zulu empire was expanding and consolidating its power and for three-quarters of a century conditions were quite unstable.

Nevertheless, the construction of Natal's first railway at Durban in 1860 led to schemes for additional lines. The first portion of the future North Coast Railway, opened to Umgeni in 1867, was built to a gauge of 4' 8½", and the story of its conversion to 3' 6" was similar to that of the Cape Main Line. 'Broad gauge' was fine at the coast, but when the route inland was planned the narrow gauge was chosen for economic reasons, and the existing wide gauge followed suit. The opening of the extension to Verulam in 1879 coincided with the narrowing of the rails and South Africa's 'standard gauge' was a *fait accompli*.

Verulam remained the terminus for 18 years, until coal deposits deep in Zululand at Somkele (near present-day Mtubatuba) provided the motive for extending the railway northwards and parallel to the coast. The Tugela extension was opened in 1897 under the auspices of the Zululand Railway Company, and soon afterwards a 1 330-foot bridge was built over the river by the Government railways who completed construction to Somkele in 1903.

The coal at Somkele proved to be of mediocre quality, but the mines remained in operation until the mid-1920s when the line was extended from Mtubatuba up the coast but well inland, reaching the Swaziland border at Golela in 1927. Today there is a flurry of activity as work proceeds on an extension into Swaziland and the link-up with the Swaziland Railway. In theory at least, it will be possible to travel by rail from Durban to Maputo (Lourenço Marques), roughly following the route taken by survivors of many shipwrecks recorded in the early history of Natal.

212

212 Passenger traffic to Zululand has always been heavy, and two daily trains run in each direction to Empangeni. For many years the GF Garratts and 14R 4-8-2s were the regular performers, but with improvements to the line in the early 1960s heavier locomotives could be used. In 1964, a dozen each of Classes 15CA and CB arrived at Greyville from the Transvaal, and they operated up the coast until electrification reached Mandini in 1972. Here a 15CA named 'Duguza' leaves Gingingdlovu on its way to Empangeni with Train No. 291.

213 The final Garratt classes to operate in Zululand were the GMA and GO double-Mountains, both types transferred there after 1970. When this photograph was taken in June 1975, the electrification to Empangeni had just been completed and diesels were already making forays up the coast to Mtubatuba. The train is No. 3741, a Sundays-only passenger between Empangeni and Golela and the locomotive is a GO. Within months the GOs were on their way to De Aar where they have been stored ever since – a sad ending for SAR's last Garratt class.

214 Before 14Rs, 15CAs and 15CBs came into use in the 1960s, Garratts were the mainstay of the North Coast. They continued to be useful there right to the end, and when this GE departed from Stanger with a goods train for Durban during 1968 there were five classes of Garratt in operation along the line.

214

In Zululand

215 It's midday on a lazy Sunday in 1969. As the melodic Zulu singing from the small church hidden in the trees reaches a crescendo we first hear the distant laboured exhaust of an engine working its way up the steep grade from the Mhlatuzi River at Felixton. Soon the singing is drowned by the sound of a 14R which fills the forest, echoing off the tall trees which encroach on the railway. Working clean-stacked, the 4-8-2 advances steadily, its 48″ drivers holding firm on the track. The turbulent exhaust from the engine reaches the underside of the bridge with a clap which shakes the earth, and then she's upon us, leaning into the curve. The tin roof of the church vibrates and rattles until the train is past, and the sound of the guard's van clicking on the joints recedes into the distance. Now the noise from the engine's exhaust is lost in the forest and all is quiet. Even the singing has stopped.

216 The five GDAs were elusive and seldom photographed. Though branch-line machines, they were occasionally seen out on the North Coast Main Line. No. 2256 is here leaving Darnall in January 1968 and from this angle the odd design of rear water tank and coal bunker is clearly visible. These locomotives were the bar-framed equivalents of the earlier GDs.

217 Largest steam locomotive to work in Zululand, the GL, is seen on a long train made up largely of empty BA wagons which will return filled with cut poles for the Free State and Transvaal mines. The location is the recently-doubled line from Amatikulu, soon to be draped with catenary. When these GLs arrived on the North Coast in 1969, they caused quite a stir. They were by far the largest engines many drivers had ever seen, and in the hot North Coast climate they were devils to work on.

218

Up to Eshowe

On the road map of Zululand the main road from Gingindlovu to Eshowe runs in an almost straight line, and the railway (not shown on all maps) wriggles only slightly. What the road map doesn't show is that both road and rail climb an escarpment, gaining over 1 500 feet in the process! From the timetable which gives station altitudes, it can be calculated that in the first eight miles the line gains 279 feet, while in the last 12 the climb is 1 229 feet. A profile diagram from the Civil Engineer's office adds the final pieces of information: the ruling grade is 1 in 40, and there are 108 curves in all.

We first investigated this interesting route early in 1968. After driving overnight from Johannesburg, we turned off onto the narrow track following the railway to Dikinyana. It was already light on a thickly overcast morning. A GE Garratt was struggling

on an uphill train round a tight curve, flanges squealing, wheels slipping. The engine soon stalled, and was dragged back several feet by the weight of its own train. Straining to regain uphill momentum, it spun its wheels time and again.

By now the fireman was running ahead of the locomotive, sanding the rails by hand as he went. The driver was leaning out of the cab as far as he could, holding the throttle with one hand and resting the other on the window elbow-rest. He took slack once again and after some smart work with the regulator the train took hold on the sanded rail. Soon it was moving, but very slowly, and the fireman clambered back into the cab as the train gradually gathered speed up the hill. We stood in the morning drizzle completely absorbed by this tussle between man, machine and environment.

220

219

218 Late on a winter's afternoon the hills of Zululand seem to take on an extra dimension in the cross lighting of the low sun as this GO twists its bulk around a sharp curve between Bumba and Dikinyana. These GOs were the only mechanically-fired Garratts to run on the Eshowe branch, but after a short spell in 1975 they were taken off as they tended to start fires in the cane fields.

219 Heading for the mills at Amatikulu, a GO eases a full load of cane down the 1 in 40 to Gingindlovu.

220 At Huletts siding a train of empty cane wagons works towards Eshowe. The engine, a GEA, was the last steam class to operate on the line. For a time the GEAs were supplemented by GOs, but being hand-fired they had less of a tendency to throw sparks than the mechanically-stoked GOs and so they returned in force some months before dieselisation.

177

221

Nkwalini Branch

221 Heatonville is a typical South African country station, with its corrugated iron buildings, windmill and rows of cultivated trees. In this scene, loaded cane wagons wait while GE No. 2262 shunts off a wagon before continuing on her way back to Empangeni.

222 Nearing the end of her days, the first GE, No. 2260, works freight on the Nkwalini branch in 1971. These engines were South Africa's first eight-coupled Garratts, and after years of service on the Krugersdorp-Mafeking line they were transferred to Natal, mainly for service up the North Coast. Electrification and the arrival of GMAs and GOs pushed them off the main line by 1970, and their last service was on this branch. In a final effort to utilise the GEs, the SAR sent one up to the Utrecht branch where it doubled the loads of 19As, but re-laying of the line a few months later meant that 15Fs could be used.

222

1970's Coal Line

Railways are alive and well and still expanding in South Africa. Two of the biggest projects in recent years were the Saldanha Bay iron-ore line and the Richards Bay coal line. Between them, they have added 735 route miles to SAR's domain but they leave steam enthusiasts cold – diesel traction was used at first, and now electric locomotives pull the unit-loads on these heavy-duty lines. Steam was used during the construction of the Richards Bay line, and water facilities were even installed en route! Ballast and construction trains ran the length of the new line, and for a short time it was possible to photograph steam on what is now a non-steam railway.

223 Highest 3′ 6″ railway bridge in South Africa is this huge concrete structure which spans the White Umfolozi River, not far from historic Ulundi, the old Zulu imperial capital and the present capital of KwaZulu. This steam train, in fact any train, looks like a toy on the massive structure.

223

Lilliputian Line

224 Driver Bill Bester takes great pride in his 2'-gauge Garratt, appropriately named 'Lilliputian'. He makes a return trip every day on the Estcourt–Weenen branch, most northerly of Natal's SAR narrow-gauge lines. Passengers are conveyed in small carriages attached to the normal goods train, effectively making it a mixed.

225 Cleaning the firebox of a NGG13 Garratt is not difficult: the grate area is only 19½ square feet.

224
225

11 North Natal Coal Lines

South Africa has been blessed with some of the largest coal deposits in the world. There are deposits in every province, but only Natal and the Transvaal have high-grade coal. Much of Natal's is semi-anthracite and a good portion of this is suitable for coking purposes. What is not consumed locally by ISCOR (Iron & Steel Industrial Corporation) is exported, although, strangely enough, South Africa has to import certain grades of coking coal.

The Natal coal belt stretches from north of Ladysmith to Newcastle and east from Utrecht to Hlobane, and commercial exploitation dates back over 100 years. When the NGR main line was being extended northwards a branch was constructed to Talana to serve the mines, and this later became part of the through route to Vryheid and Hlobane, a major coal-producing area. A second line running from Newcastle to Utrecht was opened in 1910. The Glencoe-Vryheid line went electric in 1968 but the Newcastle-Utrecht line remained steam into 1978, although plans call for dieselization in the near future.

For many years the Utrecht branch had the special appeal of a branch line with smaller engines predominating, but the Glencoe-Vryheid line supported the weight of much larger main-line type engines including the famous GL Garratts. When these engines, designed as a stopgap for the lower Natal Main Line, were introduced in 1929, they more than doubled the load of two 14R 4-8-2s. In 1938 they were transferred to Glencoe and for the next 30 years this was their home. They established themselves as the finest drag steam engines on the SAR, working 1 250-ton trains up the long 1 in 50 uncompensated grades, and it seems a great pity that the SAR never developed this type into a modern high speed machine for its main lines.

226 Lasting well into the 1970s, steam on the Utrecht branch is now of the main-line type and a stud of 15Fs, often double-headed, runs the traffic. Here we see a train leaving Newcastle with the steelworks in the background.

227 Back in 1965 Victor Hand photographed GL No. 2350 working loaded coal out of Tayside. It was normal for these great machines to run bunker first, a practice that dated back to Natal Main Line days when the many tunnels made crew comfort essential. These were the first SAR engines to be equipped with smoke-deflecting cowls, a feature of later GMAM Garratts.

226

The Enyati Railway

A large number of private industrial railways have operated in South Africa over the years. All have been interesting, some for their locomotives and some for their mode of operating. It is a joy to find a railway combining these attractions, and for this there is none to compare with the Enyati Railway which operates a 14-mile main line in the Hlobane coalfield. The setting is beautiful. From the SAR junction at Boomlaer the line climbs the north face of Inyati Ridge on a ruling gradient of 1 in 50, almost encircling Pondwana Mountain, to a neck formed by the intersection of the Inyati (buffalo) and Ngwibi Ridges. From this point one can see the headwaters of two of Natal's great rivers, the Mkuze in the north and the Black Umfolozi in the south. It is also possible to see two of the three collieries responsible for the railway's continued existence: the Natal Ammonium Mine on the north face of Mount Ngwibi and the Enyati Mine on the eastern flank of Mount Inyati. The Natal Anthracite Mine, on the opposite side of the valley from Enyati, is just out of sight but very much in evidence as a four-mile ropeway brings the coal to a loading point at the Enyati Mine.

Rider Haggard once stood here, gazing down into the Umfolozi Valley – the Valley of Mist – and he is said to have gained inspiration here for one of his African novels. In this lovely setting the railway enthusiast will find a line which is completely steam-worked, boasting a roster of ten locomotives, four or five of which can be seen in action at any one time.

228 Three Garratts – that's 12 cylinders, 18 sets of coupled wheels and a combined tractive force of nearly 120 000 lbs for a total engine weight of 435 tons! Enyati operates a mountain-climbing railway big in everything but length, where it is possible to see articulated engines double-heading, banking, and even triple-heading as in this photo. Pat Lovell, the genial manager of Enyati's railway, is an old Great Western man who after many years as a driver in Rhodesia has Garratts in his blood. He has five ex-SAR GF Garratts and one ex-RR 16th Class Garratt to make him a very happy man.

229 The only Decapod (2-10-0) to run in South Africa, Enyati No. 4, started life as a 2-10-2 T, outshopped by Baldwin in 1936. She was one of two such engines operated by Enyati. Her sister was scrapped, but she was rebuilt to this tank-tender configuration in 1975 and a year later she was very much in service, though not a popular engine. She is seen here double-heading with 4-8-2 No. 3 in 1976. Since 1976, Dunn's of Witbank have supplied their own locomotives to supplement the Enyati engines, and today the operation is largely in the hands of Garratts.

230 Double-banking, very rare for South Africa, has happened several times at Enyati usually during bad weather. Loaded trains leaving the neck for Boomlaer normally have one banker, but on this trip RR Garratt 618 was assisted by Baldwin 2-10-0 No. 4 and ex-SAR 14th Class No. 3. In the middle foreground is a 14R, leased from SAR, which had been involved in a rear-end collision several weeks previously. It conveniently rolled over onto its side, leaving the line clear and causing hardly any damage to the track.

231

231 Former SAR and RR locomotives pair up to move empties at the neck. The leading engine, one of four Class 1 4-8-0s (ex-NGR Hendrie 'B's), owned by Enyati, was the last still operating, in 1977. The rear engine is the ex-RR Class 16, built by Beyer Peacock in 1929.

232 Locomotive purists revere Enyati's No. 3. She is the last of the classic Hendrie 14th Class 4-8-2s still in unrebuilt form (all SAR 14s have been re-boilered and classified 14R). ISCOR originally bought her from the SAR for their Pretoria steelworks in 1942. When they dieselised in the early sixties she was sold to Enyati; but before long she came due for overhaul. After a narrow escape from the scrappers' torch, she was revived in 1969 and has been running ever since. SAR now wants to buy her for their railway museum, but for the time being one can still enjoy the sight of her working in the province for which she was designed over 60 years ago.

233 Baldwin No. 4 arrives at the neck with empties for the Ngwibi Colliery while the former RR Garratt stands by with loads from the Natal Anthracite Mine.

234 Vryheid Coronation operates one diesel and five steam locomotives, three of them Standard North British 4-8-4Ts. The diesel normally works the main line, but on this day early in 1978 two 4-8-4Ts deputise for it on a train of coke near the SAR interchange at Hlobane.

235 *Stylish Garratt.* In 1969 Hlobane Colliery's ex-SAR GCA was rebuilt with new tanks front and rear and nicknamed GCB, but she didn't last long before being scrapped. Neighbouring Vryheid Coronation had two GCAs at one time, but they too have gone. In fact, there are no longer any GCAs in regular service, as SAR's last examples were withdrawn during 1976, and all those sold earlier into private use have also been retired.

236 This massive 2-10-2T is one-of-a-kind, built for Hlobane Colliery by Baldwin in 1930 and known as the 'Vryheid' type. Although in reserve for a new diesel, she will probably see several more years of service. She is painted black now, but back in 1969 she was photographed in ex-works condition.

237 Non-articulated and articulated tanks couple to move a short train up a steep incline at the Coronation Colliery. Garratts are really tank engines, although many enthusiasts do not think of them as such. All GEA Garratts have now been withdrawn from SAR service. No. 5, an ex-SAR GEA Class was the only example operating at the beginning of 1978. Resplendent in a new coat of blue paint, she's smarter than when she was SAR property.

238 At Durnacol is another private railway which has been revitalized by recent expansion programmes to provide additional coking coal for the ISCOR plants at Newcastle, Vanderbijlpark and Pretoria. The original mine produced bunker coal for ships at Durban: hence its full name, Durban Navigation Colliery. It has been in operation for nearly 75 years, and the opening of a new mine has made another 75 years of operation a possibility. To service the new mine, the existing four-mile line has been extended by four miles. The mine's first locomotives, three Class 1 4-8-0s, have been retired and four new and larger engines have taken their place. One is an ex-RR Class 16 Garratt, equipped by Dunn's with a Giesl ejector; the second is an ex-SAR GM Garratt; the third – rather a rose among the thorns – is an ex-SAR 16CR Pacific; and the fourth is an ex-SAR 15E 4-8-2. The 15E with her poppet valves may seem out of place in an operation of this sort, but she still puts in a good day's work. Here we see the 15E and GM working together to take a train from No. 7 shaft to Dannhauser station.

239 Gieslised Garratt. Durnacol runs South Africa's only operating locomotive equipped with this exhaust-ejector. Unfortunately, in short-run colliery service this apparatus has had little effect on coal consumption.

240 Newcastle-Platberg operates its mine near Elandslaagte, and a three-mile spur connects it to the SAR station there. It has run a variety of ex-SAR tank engines as well as a 6th Class 4-6-0, but its last tank engine was a converted standard North British product, seen here rebuilt as a tank-tender. More recently, two ex-SAR 19A 4-8-2s have taken over.

241 Of only three 4-8-2 tank locomotives built by Hawthorne Leslie for South Africa, two were built in 1937 for Phoenix Colliery near Witbank. They worked there until the mine closed in 1967, then disappeared and were presumed scrapped. But later they reappeared at the Natal-Cambrian Colliery at Ballengeich where they still run.

240   241

12 Western Transvaal Highveld

The Reef

Old Jock Campbell knew how to run! His engine, 16C No. 824, was the pride of the Pretoria link. Jock's ancestry showed in the Scottish thistles adorning the smokebox door. Mike Callaghan, his fireman, helped with the spit and polish while keeping up steam – and they went as far as burnishing parts that other crews would only paint. To let people know who was coming, 824's number was carried in gold leaf on her red buffer beam.

In Jock's day, six- to eight-coach trains were standard on the Pretoria-Jo'burg run and the Hendrie 16th Class Pacifics were the star performers. Trains would leave Pretoria at a smart pace, reeling off onto the right-hand single track under the old signal gantry which spanned several tracks, and charging up the immediate 1 in 67. Gaining speed up the hill, the engine would literally lean outwards as it rounded the 492-foot horseshoe in Fountains Valley, then accelerate rapidly on the short 1 in 500 through Ashbury and up the bank to Lyttleton (now Verwoerdburg). Here, a slight downgrade would enable her to pick up more speed and roar through Irene at over 50 mph, in anticipation of the eight-mile 1 in 66 to Kaalfontein. Even at the top of this bank speed would often exceed 40 mph, and the less demanding stretch to Elandsfontein would bring it above 50 mph again.

Three miles of level and descending track to Driefontein followed. Here it was difficult to hold the maximum allowed speed of 55 mph but no free running was permissible, particularly as the pronounced descent with tight curves into Germiston required some smart enginemanship for a smooth and punctual arrival.

From Germiston the train would start out over the four-track main on its last nine miles to Johannesburg: past Driehoek, then through the sweeping curves between the old Simmer & Jack goldmine dumps, through Cleveland, Denver and George Goch, and into Jeppe and Doornfontein where speed had to be checked for the final approach to Jo'burg.

These express trains between the nation's administrative capital and its largest city set standards that stood for many years. Not only did the 45-mile run from Pretoria involve a climb of over 1 200 feet but in those days the first 36 miles were nearly all single track. Nevertheless, 'express' trains – which made two stops – were scheduled to take one hour and 15 minutes. This timing was eased after electrification in 1938 and was not improved upon until 1973 when a non-stop train was introduced experimentally for two years. This train took 64 minutes over a line which is multiple-tracked throughout and has been straightened a great deal since 1938.

The Pretoria-Johannesburg line is but one of a huge network of lines within a 50-mile radius of the golden city. They had an austere beginning in 1890 when the 16-mile 'Randtram' with its tiny tank engines and short coffin-like coaches began operating between Johannesburg and Boksburg. Since then the railways of the Transvaal Highveld have expanded to become the most densely trafficked in South Africa.

The opening up of the goldfields in President Kruger's South African Republic during 1886 raised the question of a railway to the sea. The Boers feared that this would bring the British whose influence they had trekked north to avoid, so to forestall dependence on the colonial railways which were reaching for the Witwatersrand from the south, they decided to build a railway of their own. This was the Delagoa Bay line which was to head eastwards to the border of Moçambique and down to the then small port of Lourenço Marques. The story of this railway (the Nederlandsche Zuid-Afrikaansche Spoorwegmaatschappij, later just the ZASM) was fraught with political and financial intrigue, and there were so many delays that the Republican Government eventually had to sanction the southern connection. The line to Cape Town via the Free State was opened in 1892, two years before the Delagoa Bay line finally reached Pretoria, and the Durban connection was completed in 1895. Thus the groundwork was laid for a unified South African railway system.

The Transvaal, with 23% of South Africa's land area, contains 30% of its railway mileage and has the largest portion of originating traffic, particularly for coal and minerals. At the end of 1977 over 35% of its route mileage was electrified (compared with an average of under 25% for South Africa as a whole), including the intensive suburban service along the Reef and from Pretoria. Although many of the more important non-electrified lines have been dieselised, a sizeable number of steam locomotives remain at work on secondary and branch lines. However, the bulk are engaged in shunting and hauler work under the wires on the Witwatersrand. Five main sheds (Millsite, Germiston, Kazerne, Springs and Capital Park: all within a 50-mile radius) are home for nearly 300 of the 500 engines that operate in the province. Present plans call for the continued use of steam on the Reef, and it could very well be that the last steam locomotives to operate in South Africa will be in the Transvaal.

242

242 Just before the 6.55 pm train departure time at Johannesburg, Pacific 824, immaculate as always, waits for the signal to take Train No. 625 to Pretoria. Back in the mid-30s, when action photography was rare and night-time rail photography even rarer, Frank Garrison took this beautiful shot of Jock Campbell's engine.

243 Oldtimers would not recognise Johannesburg station today. Steam has not appeared on regular trains since 1959, when the decking over the new station was completed. For a full decade steam was absent from the station, only approaching the western end of the platforms in shunting movements from Braamfontein yard. Then on April 11, 1969 a Blue Train special was run from Johannesburg to Cape Town to celebrate the 30th anniversary of the air-conditioned Blue Train. The engine, 16E No. 855, pulled the train to Klerksdorp on the direct route to Cape Town which was opened in 1906 and is today used by most of the important trains between the two centres.

243

245

244 The Germiston station pilot is a 12R 4-8-2, immaculate both inside and out.

245 In Kazerne yard, on the south side of Jo'burg, heavy shunting goes on 24 hours a day. It is the Reef's only hump yard, and back in 1970 three very clean 12ARs were reserved for the job of pushing long rakes of cars at very low speed over the top. This engine was the 'Kobus Loubser', namesake of the present SAR General Manager. His father, Dr M. M. Loubser who was Chief Mechanical Engineer from 1939 to 1949, designed the massive boiler fitted to 44 of the 67 12A 4-8-2s when they were re-boilered and reclassified 12AR.

246 On the Witwatersrand, gold mining came first and the railways followed soon afterwards. From east to west along this golden arc, railways and mines intermingle, main lines and shunting spurs twisting around high mine dumps. Drifting sand blows down from the dumps onto passing trains, but a grass has been found which will grow in the chemically-treated sand. This has now covered many of the dumps, making them less of a nuisance but also less picturesque, and we were fortunate to have an ungrassed dump as the background for this Class S shunter at the Germiston railway yards.

247 Now extinct on SAR rails, the 14 Class S 0-8-0s, built by Henschel in 1928-9, were the first purely shunting locomotives designed for the SAR. They were retired in 1976, and some have since been sold for service on the mines. In July 1976 No. 369, the last of its class still in SAR service, was photographed shunting on a spur near Roodepoort.

248

The Krugersdorp-Mafeking Line

On Mondays and Fridays, promptly at 12.30 pm a train would pull out of Jo'burg station, heading west under the catenary. This train was unique in South Africa since it was composed largely of Rhodesian Railways coaches, their near Great Western Railway colours of chocolate and cream looking distinguished in comparison with the SAR's gulf red and quaker grey. 26 hours and 674 miles later the train would slide into Bulawayo, having covered 206 miles of South African territory, 400 miles in Botswana and a final 68 miles in Rhodesia.

The South African portion through the Western Transvaal Highveld between Krugersdorp and Mafeking was really a mountain railway with its numerous 1 in 40 grades and almost continuous climbs of up to 20 miles. Until dieselization of the South African section early in 1972, all but the short electrified Johannesburg–Krugersdorp section was in the hands of Garratts, Rhodesian and South African. As of April 1978, the RR coaches ceased to enter South Africa, and the Botswana Government is expected to take over the Rhodesian property in their territory before long, thus ending another era.

This line was for many years the important bridge route between the Reef industrial complex and Rhodesia, for it formed part of the only through railway between the two countries. In 1975, Beit Bridge in the Northern Transvaal was linked up with Rutenga on the Gwelo-Malvernia line in Rhodesia, and most freight traffic now moves directly between the two countries.

The Krugersdorp-Mafeking section, one of the more difficult secondary lines in the country to operate because of the grades and also because of traffic density, was an early testing-ground for Garratts. SAR's first double-eight coupled Garratts, the GEs, saw many years' service here, as did the less powerful GFs. Then in 1938 the final stage in the evolution of branch-line Garratts began with the introduction of the GM 4-8-2 + 2-8-4s. The 16 engines in this class were to spend nearly their whole lives here, in later years assisted by the GMAs, their lineal descendants.

248 Meet of GM and GMA at Ottoshoop in December 1971 when the Transvaal was in the vivid green of midsummer.

249 Shortly before GMs were displaced from the Mafeking line, this one worked the westbound Rhodesia Express past the old York mine dump at Krugersdorp. The train is already on the single track of the Mafeking line which here runs parallel to the electrified Potchefstroom – Kimberley main line.

250 On September 19, 1971, GM No. 2295 and GMA No. 4102 team up to move a westbound ballast train up the grade from Magaliesburg station. Six months later, the 16 GMs and 21 GMAs were gone from Millsite shed. Some were transferred to other duties, but sadly the majority of GMs saw no further service.

250

c

253

254

Industrials

Industrial railways once abounded in the Transvaal and Northern Free State, with a variety of motive power unequalled in all Africa. Engines were to be seen at quaint and often decrepit small sheds in the shade of goldmine dumps and under pit headgears, but 'progress' has caught up with these railways and many have been closed while others have converted to internal combustion traction.

255

251 On the roster of ESCOM (the Electricity Supply Commission) is 'Hunslet', a 2-6-0 T built in 1902 and still active in 1978.

252 ESCOM also operates this old lady, a former Natal Government Railways engine, built by Kitson in 1879 – perhaps to be South Africa's first working centenarian locomotive.

253 Cornelia Colliery at Viljoensdrif in the Northern Free State operates this perfectly turned out North British 4-8-2 T.

254 Numberplate from Rustenburg Platinum Mine's No. 1, a 2'-gauge 0-4-2 T, built by Bagnall in 1906.

255 Daggafontein Mine operated this old 'Dubs A' 4-8-2 T, constructed in 1900 for the NGR.

256 An unusual 2-6-0 T, built by Andrew Barclay in 1951 for Klipfontein Organic Products.

257 There were 175 locomotives in the famous ZASM 'B' Class. The last regularly operating members ran on Government Gold Mines which closed in 1971.

258 Still working on Grootvlei Proprietary Mine are two old 'Dubs A' tank engines, amongst the last to be running in South Africa. The mine has recently added an ex-SAR Class S 0-8-0 tender engine to its roster.

259 Sub-Nigel had three small engines on its 2' 6" line in the East Rand, including No. 2, a 1926 Hudswell Clarke 0-4-2 T.

260 East Rand Proprietary Mine operated one of the largest industrial railway systems on the Reef, and in steam days it boasted no fewer than nine locomotives. No. 10 is the 4-8-4 variation of the standard North British tank engine.

Gold Carrier: REGM

Steve Verster sits at the desk in his small office, photos of his engines and a large map of his empire on the walls. 'We're pulling more reef each month now,' he says. 'Yes man, I know, it's a pity that the diesels get most of the work – a 15BR can run the pants off a diesel any day. But when the diesels are in for servicing, our steam is out again and doing a great job too. The youngest is getting on for 60 – not bad for any locomotive.'

Mr Verster is the manager of Randfontein Estates Gold Mine's ore-carrying railway, and he is unashamedly a steam man. His railway began its life under steam and would probably have remained so but for a quirk of fate. The parent company, a large Johannesburg mining house, cancelled the development of a new platinum mine when the price of the metal dropped in 1976. This left it with two surplus diesels which were sent to REGM. The company was anxious to get the most service from these expensive units, and they now handle the bulk of the traffic. But they are small shunting units – hardly a match for even a medium-size steam engine – and their slow 10 mph grind uphill is hardly exciting compared to the 25 mph gait of a 15BR.

REGM was for many years one of the largest gold mining operations on the Reef, but during the early 1960s mining was curtailed and only a skeleton operation remained. Then in 1971 it was announced that a new mining area was to be developed, but most interesting was the news that a new six-mile railway was to be constructed to the new mine at Cooke Section.

This shaft was in a hollow which meant that reef would have to be pulled uphill for nine miles to the existing reduction plant. It was too much to expect the small tank engines still on the property to do such work. Something larger was needed: not diesels, but steam! First to arrive were two Class 1 4-8-0s and two 15BR 4-8-2s. After a Class 1 and a 15BR were badly damaged in an accident, two more 15BRs were purchased. When the engines emerged from shops, they were dazzling in a livery of blue with yellow trim. Then came the diesels, and although at least one steam engine operates each day, the future is in doubt. Another shaft has been opened (Cooke No. 2) and a new reduction plant is being built at the far end of the line. This will probably mean the end of the long ore haul and the relegation of the railway to stores use only – very sad for those of us who saw this short-lived operation in its prime.

261 It's a rare winter morning in the Highveld that breaks both clear and perfectly still. When this banked train came into view halfway up the hill from Cooke Shaft, its steam and smoke trail formed a path right back to the mine shaft. Incidentally, each of the 12 ore wagons carries over R7 000 in recoverable gold.

262 Like their tank-engine predecessors, REGM's current locomotives are painted blue. An SAR engine, Class 15BR, painted black for the first 55 years of its life but now painted Caledonian blue is worth travelling a long way to see! REGM No. 2 climbs past old mine dumps, massive pyramids on the horizon.

261

262

263 Minutes after sunrise, a banked train begins to move at Cooke Shaft, its two ex-SAR 15BR 4-8-2s exhausting a mixture of steam and coal smoke into an almost windless sky. Steam trains are usually loaded up to seven or eight full ore wagons, but at the end of the night shift, when the Cooke Shaft shunter returns to the loco shed at the other end of the line, he will often bank a train on the way, increasing the payload in the process.

264 *Designs worlds apart.* This view of REGM's ex-SAR locomotives shows very different design philosophies: the lead engine, a Class 1 with low running boards, small wheels and low-pitched boiler, is typical of David Hendrie's British-rooted ideas, while the Canadian-built 15BR directly behind has large wheels, a high-pitched boiler and high running boards. Though the Class 1 may look smaller than the 15BR, it is the more powerful locomotive in terms of tractive effort – but the 15BR would outdo it in terms of horsepower output.

265 Passenger trains on mine railways are more the exception than the rule, and it was interesting news when REGM purchased some SAR suburban coaches and started running four passenger trains each day. Unfortunately they didn't last long: ore traffic became so heavy that it was decided to transport the miners by road.

266 In the days of the tank engines REGM had nine until the mid-1960s when four of the older ones were scrapped. This left four 'Improved Dubs B' engines and one standard North British product — all 4-8-2Ts. Some of these engines were used in the construction of the Cooke Shaft line and even to haul reef before the arrival of ex-SAR tender engines, and here we see No. 4, its slant cylinders a significant feature. All REGM's tank engines have now been disposed of, some returning to service on other industrial lines.

265

East Rand

Surviving SAR steam on the Witwatersrand appears in greatest strength as one travels east from Johannesburg. Germiston comes first and its 121 locomotives (as of December 1977) work mostly under the wires in shunting, trip, and hauler work along the Reef. Further east, Springs has perhaps the most interesting shed on the Reef. When steam has fast been disappearing from SAR rails, it is surprising to see a depot where the steam allocation has been increasing. From 28 engines late in 1969 the shed allocation had increased to 57 by the end of 1977. Most of the Springs locomotives are confined to shunting and hauler work along the East Rand, but there is a sizeable amount of traffic on the non-electrified secondary main line to Breyten and all this activity is expected to continue for some time. In fact the steam allocation at Springs is to be increased gradually during the next few years.

267 Largest shunting locomotives on the SAR are the 37 Class S1 0-8-0s, constructed between 1947 and 1954, and unusual in that the first 12 were built in South Africa. SAR never built its own locomotives in great numbers, preferring to import them. Springs shed has one of these engines, seen here on the daily abattoir train.

268 The last steam suburban service on the Reef, between Springs and Nigel, finally went over to electric traction in February 1976. Mainstay of the service during the last few years were the 24th Class 2-8-4s. On the six-coach, swing-door sets which were standard for the line, their phenomenal powers of acceleration made them a match for the multiple-unit electric sets which replaced them. Here a 24 makes a fine start from Dunnottar station on a frosty morning in July 1974.

269 When a 15F on the daily freight from Heidelberg stalled on the stiff climb between Selpark and Springs, an S Class 0-8-0 came to the rescue. In the winter twilight they are seen in silhouette against the western sky.

268

269

209

13 Eastern Highveld and Escarpment

Bridge Route

270 The date is October 18, 1976. The very last steam passenger train from Breyten to Vryheid has crossed the border between the Transvaal and Natal near Commondale and now sweeps around a gentle curve on the new alignment north of Paulpietersburg.

271 An hour later the same train has left the new line and is following the old route down to the water stop at Bivane. The GMAM has filled its auxiliary tank in preparation for the 21-mile climb to Tendeka, and from there it will travel the Hlobane branch on the last nine miles into Vryheid. The next day the new line was opened, bypassing the Bivane waterpoint, and so all trains were of necessity diesel-powered.

272 Only minutes have passed since the morning mist cleared from the valley and the dew is still heavy on the grass as two 12As make a stunning entrance, climbing up from Machadodorp towards Breyten in December 1977. This line is usually worked by GMA Garratts, but 15ARs and 15CAs assisted during the early 1970s; these 12As were the usual shunting engines at Waterval Boven until transferred to De Aar in February 1978.

The Machadodorp-Vryheid line along the Eastern Transvaal escarpment is an important link between the Eastern Main Line and the coal-producing areas of Northern Natal. The line carried plenty of traffic, but it always had a definite branch-line character. Dramatic change came in 1976 with the completion of the Richards Bay coal line from Broodsnyersplaas (former terminus of the branch from Ogies) to the Natal coast. Much of the coal line is completely new, but between Ermelo and Vryheid it closely parallels and in some places uses the original formation. Long unit-loads of coal move behind the electric locomotives which have recently replaced the diesels which were first used in this service.

Lowveld Branches

The hills of the Eastern Transvaal Lowveld drew prospectors from all over the world during the great gold rushes of the 1870s and 1880s. The first big strikes were in the Pilgrim's Rest area, and the biggest of all was in 1880 in De Kaap Valley near where the town of Barberton is today.

After the excitement of the gold rushes died down, the arrival of the Delagoa Bay Railway in the 1890s heralded a new rush, this time to farm semi-tropical fruit in the hot valleys. Later, the high rainfall along the berg encouraged the cultivation of large plantations of wattle, and of pines which come to maturity in the incredibly short time of seven or eight years.

First branch off the main line was the Kaapmuiden-Barberton line, completed in 1896. Station names such as Revolver Creek, Eureka, and Joe's Luck bear witness to the area's colourful past, and the last major working gold mine, the Sheba Mine, lies along this line. The Nelspruit-Graskop branch came later, reaching Sabie in 1913 and Graskop the following year. Another short branch from this line was completed to Plaston in 1926. Both these lines serve large citrus farms in the lower reaches, but the main traffic is from timber plantations located further up along the foothills of the Transvaal Drakensberg.

274

273 The Graskop branch goes right over the mountains on a ruling grade of 1 in 40 compensated. GCA and GF Garratts were the regular power here for many years, and in 1968 Nelspruit's allocation included three GCAs and 17 GFs. The GFs averaged over 2 000 miles a month per locomotive: no mean feat for a short mountainous railway. Sadly, when the SAR announced its 'total steam elimination' programme in 1972, the Graskop branch was one of the first to go, yielding to the diesel in May 1973. On 5 May, only days before the end, blue GF No. 2401 'Magdalena' works a southbound freight from Sabie through the forests to the summit at Spitskop. This famous engine was kept spotless by driver Van Staden – whose white safari suit remained spotless throughout his shift.

274 It's the end of winter and the bushveld is parched and bleak. In September 1969, a rare combination of motive power fronts this train leaving Kaapmuiden for Barberton. The GF leading the 19D was on loan from Nelspruit.

275 For the historians: Waterval Onder as it used to be, with the old ZASM roundhouse full of ZASM 'B' tank engines, waiting their turn to tackle the hill. The rack engines must have been out working.

276 Detail of a GMAM cowl, designed for tunnel operation. The deflection plate could be drawn over the chimney to drive the smoke and cinders down alongside the train, but it was a controversial device and not many drivers used it.

277 A bunker-first GMAM leads a 15F downgrade between Waterval Boven and Ondervalle in September 1965.

278 After the electricity was turned on late in April 1966, steam, diesel and electric locomotives were all used for a time. Here GMAM No. 4070 arrives at Ondervalle, site of an unusual arrangement of passing tracks similar to that at Tunnel on Hex River Pass where crossing space is also at a premium. Two dead-end tracks faced uphill traffic, one faced downhill, and all were level so that trains would not have to be re-started on steep grades. Beyond to Waterval Boven, the line had been doubled only months before, causing a bad bottleneck here. Often all three sidings were full, with two or three more trains out on the main line. Sometimes downhill trains had to take the uphill siding and there was much see-sawing back and forth, the Garratts often letting go with sudden slips which reverberated up and down the valley.

279 The 15AR 4-8-2s were for many years the standard power on the Eastern Transvaal Main Line. The engine heading down the Elandskloof Valley from Waterval Onder is a happy reminder of the days when we would sit enjoying our midday beer at the bar opposite the eastbound water column. Just outside the door trains would be taking water, while others could be heard for up to 45 minutes as they went plodding up to the summit.

277

Over the Berg

Mountain passes have always been focal points of railway interest, and few can match the ascent of the escarpment by the Eastern Main Line between Waterval Onder and Waterval Boven. Its 1 in 50 gradient cannot compare with the 1 in 40 of Hex River and Montagu, much less with the 1 in 30 grades of Natal, nor is the length or change in altitude comparable. What does make it special is its compactness. The line runs up the side of a narrow valley as far as it can go, makes a 180 degree turn to gain altitude on the opposite side, and then does a horseshoe round a knoll in the mountain. This brings it right back nearly over itself before it climbs up the gorge through a tunnel to Ondervalle. After diving into another tunnel, the line passes a large waterfall of the Elands River, crosses the river and eventually arrives at Waterval Boven.

Until electrification in 1966, more than 80 trains ran up and down the pass each day in the Lowveld fruit season. Garratts were used, but 15CAs and 15Fs were common and before the Garratts arrived in the late fifties the smaller 12As and 15ARs were normal power. In the early days the line was the site of South Africa's only rack railway, on a grade of 1 in 20. This helped get the Delagoa Bay line over the berg in the shortest possible construction time, speeding the arrival of the first train from Lourenço Marques (now Maputo) to Pretoria, but causing a bottleneck which was not cleared until the new alignment opened in 1908.

280 A GO in midsummer on the Steelpoort line, the dark brooding sky a prelude to a heavy thunderstorm.

281 Winter white at Santa in May 1972. After spending the night here, we awoke to find the landscape covered in snow and the nearby road impassable. After hours of waiting between up and down trains, we were surprised to see a couple climbing the snow-covered slope, cameras around their necks. 'Have you come to photograph the trains?' we asked. They looked at us in utter amazement. 'Trains?' they said, 'Whatever would we want to photograph the trains for?' and then they trudged past us into the trees and disappeared into the middle of nowhere.

The Belfast-Steelpoort Line: Steam and Seasons

Railway enthusiasts tend to be interested first in the type of engine which operates on a particular line, then in the line itself and the country through which it runs. Until dieselization in 1972, SAR's last Garratt Class, the GOs, monopolized workings on the Steelpoort line. The topography and climate of this line are very interesting indeed. The northern end of the line is in the Lowveld and the lowest point is Spekboom, situated at 2 427 feet. From here the line climbs 4 448 feet to the summit at Nederhorst, which involves 75 miles of upward inclination during a 95-mile journey. This dramatic change in altitude brings dramatic changes in the climate, and the southern end of the line is subject to some of the most severe weather conditions encountered by the SAR. Heavy snowfalls are common and engines which began their journeys in the relative warmth of the lower bushveld would often encounter snowdrifts within a few hours, eventually arriving at Belfast low on coal but high on snow – literally covered with snow from one end to the other. Sometimes trains didn't make it and on occasion the line has been closed for days on end.

The Staccato Garratts

Anyone believing that the Garratt with its multitude of cylinders must sound like a whooshing Mallet, or that its twin exhausts synchronise automatically, as has been suggested by some experts, would have had his convictions shaken by a visit to the Belfast-Steelpoort line in the days of steam. The GOs stationed there had exceptionally loud sharp exhausts which seldom synchronised. The exhaust velocity was so fierce that their petticoats had to be replaced every two months because of char cutting. But given this extra bit of maintenance they were very successful machines. All 25 of this class were stationed at Lydenburg prior to dieselization in 1972.

282

282 The principal traffic on the Steelpoort line is ore from the mines in the Burgersfort and Steelpoort area, but there is also a considerable amount of general cargo – mostly livestock and timber. This train is seen leaving Santa, passing a small waterfall in the kloof.

283 The last winter the GOs fought the snowdrifts on this line: Santa, May 1972.

283

Two Highveld Branches

Two branches running north from the Eastern Transvaal Main Line have parallel histories, but their development was in opposite directions. The Cullinan branch was built to serve the famous Premier Diamond Mine, and is today a sleepy line with only one freight and two steam passenger trains from Pretoria per day. The Roossenekal branch started as a fairly quiet agricultural branch to the dorp of Stoffberg, but was extended in 1968 to serve a new mine, and has become a busy ore carrier. It has recently been electrified.

284 A 15CA leads a GMA which had been newly transferred to the Stofberg-Roossenekal line. This photograph was taken in September 1975, and within weeks most workings were taken over by Garratts which lasted until electrification early in 1977.

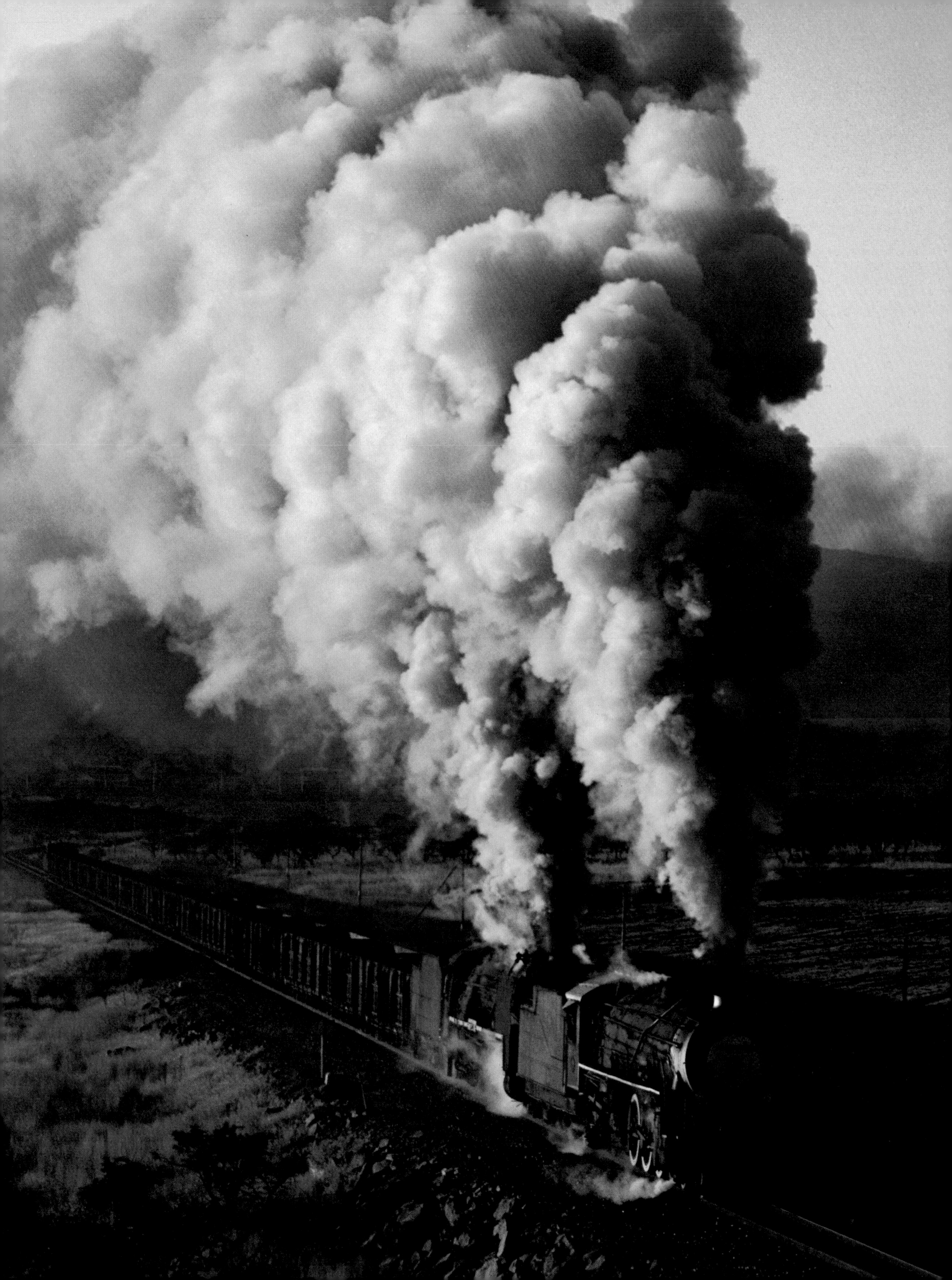

285 Departure from Roossenekal: the combination of 15CA and 15F has always been interesting as the 15CAs were the largest main-line locomotives without smoke deflectors. The value of these devices has always been doubtful, but they gave a businesslike appearance to the nearly 600 SAR engines equipped with them. The photo was taken minutes after sunrise on a freezing morning in June 1975.

286 The last steam passenger trains from Pretoria are two return suburbans working to Cullinan which operate six days a week. 15CAs are the usual power and the run includes 25 miles over the Eastern Main Line to Rayton. During October 1976, 15A No. 1791 performed on the route before being used on a number of enthusiast specials. This beautiful machine is seen leaving Cullinan where the jacarandas are in full bloom.

287 'Scorching the ballast' aptly describes 1791's departure from Rayton on its way to Cullinan in October 1976.

The Pretoria-Witbank Line: Panpoort

Station Foreman Louis van Wyk was at Panpoort station for 18 years and loved every minute. It is only 17 miles from Pretoria, but as secluded as anyone could wish. The station is in a cleft of the eastern Magaliesberg, a convenient poort used by the builders of the old Delagoa Bay Railway to bring the Eastern Main Line into Pretoria.

Louis raised a family here, living in a nearby cottage – one of three for railway personnel. Staff shortages of recent years left only two operators to man the station, working 12-hour shifts, day in and day out. On summer Sundays you could find the family Van Wyk having lunch under a small fig tree behind the station, with no distraction but the occasional station telephone call or the sounding of the Van Schoor Tablet machine which heralded yet another steam train.

Panpoort was to Pretoria what Karee was to Bloemfontein. Heavy coal traffic from Witbank, as well as timber and fruit from the Eastern Transvaal, and even imports via Lourenço Marques, flowed westwards through this poort; empty coal trucks and manufactured goods for local consumption or export moved eastwards. At the foot of a seven-mile climb of 1 in 50 to Rayton, it was the perfect place to see and hear South Africa's loudest locomotives, the 15CAs, in action.

There were few camping places to equal Panpoort. After climbing the rocky slope on the south side of the poort, we would set up camp in a good spot overlooking the east end of the loop. In summer the sun would dip behind the hillside before the Komatipoort passenger passed through, shortly after 7 pm. But the real wait was for the 'LM' Express. As darkness fell the lights of Pretoria would brighten the western sky. Through the poort we would make out a distant headlamp and if the wind was from the west we might even pick up the sound of the train's approach.

288 To photograph the westbound 'express' from Lourenço Marques one had to be up at the crack of dawn. As the two 15CAs came drifting down the grade from Rayton they opened up before the signals and left a trail of magnificent white steam in the damp air.

289 Station Foreman Louis van Wyk at the levers.

289

The Express would come wheeling into sight at about 8.20 pm, drifting down the slight grade from Pienaarspoort two miles to the west, then opening up on the curve leading into Panpoort. As the two 15CAs accelerated down the straight through the station their exhausts, already loud, echoed off the walls of the poort, filling the whole valley as if it were a giant concert hall. The headlamp shone off the rails, showing the way round the gentle curve beyond the up-home signal where the 1 in 50 climb began. They were well wound up as they passed us, the ground shaking, cinders falling around and the lights in the coaches rushing past in a blur as the express charged off into the night. Rounding a curve it disappeared from view, but reappeared three miles up the valley passing Van der Merwe, and on, out of sight. Then silence returned, but not for long: over 40 steam trains were scheduled through the poort every 24 hours and a freight would follow before long.

In mid-1977 the electricity was switched on in the recently-completed overhead, and the new CTC went into operation. Panpoort became an unmanned crossing loop and Station Foreman Van Wyk was transferred to another station. No rail enthusiasts go to Panpoort now, but those who knew it retain fond memories of this beautiful spot.

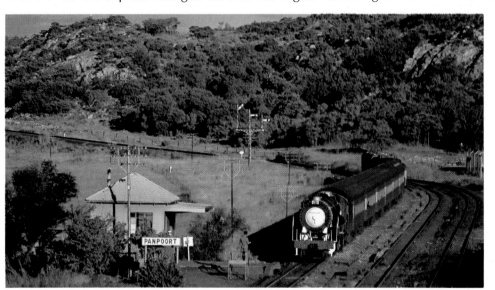

290

291

290 The daytime all-stations train from Witbank drifts into Panpoort on a summer afternoon. Local passenger trains used to stop here, but it is not listed in the public timetable and there were certainly not many passengers at this isolated spot.

291 The International Express from Lourenço Marques was normally hauled by double-headed 15CAs, but a single GMA was used for a while in the early 1970s. This engine averaged over 4 000 miles a month, but when the train loads became too heavy 15CAs took over once more. The westbound express is seen accelerating around the curve from Panpoort to Pienaarspoort soon after sunrise on 17 September 1972: the engines are 2051 and 2806.

292 A 15CA comes to grips with the 1 in 50 east of Panpoort. The smoke towers straight into the sky, then drifts down over the train, silhouetting the outer-home signal in the background.

14 Witbank Coalfields

The 800-square-mile area around Witbank lies on a solid bed of coal, and the many outcropping seams gave rise to such descriptive names as Steenkoolspruit (coal stream). But it was only when the Eastern Main Line reached Middelburg and Witbank during 1894 that commercial exploitation of the measures became possible. Now, over 80 years later, the reserves seem never-ending. Some 30 collieries are active in the area, nearly 20 operating their own railway lines which vary in length from less than a mile to several miles. Their stables of locomotives are no less varied and include a dozen classes no longer working on the SAR, as well as an assortment of industrial engines. An attractive aspect of these colliery railways is the diversity of locomotive liveries which range through many shades of green, red and blue. At the moment there is only one cloud in an otherwise bright picture – diesels are making inroads into this one-time stronghold of steam. Three collieries have capitulated in the last two years, despite the high capital costs and the necessity for expensive imported fuel and spare parts.

293 A Transvaal Navigation Colliery ex-RR Garratt in a sombre winter setting on the coalfields.

294 Beyer Peacock built three 'industrial' Garratts of the double-Prairie type between 1925 and 1935. Two worked into the 1970s, one at TNC and the other at neighbouring Clydesdale. Here the Clydesdale engine sits at the Albion loco shed midway along the TNC line during a stint as a substitute for Albion's own engines.

295 Albion Colliery shares trackage with TNC and operates a couple of small engines of its own. This de-tanked 13th Class 4-8-0 tank-tender engine is now retired but TNC has a similar engine in reserve, the last engine of its type still in operation. The 13s were rather special. They started their lives as Imperial Military Railway locomotives, built to the NGR 4-10-2T design, and during Central South African Railways administration they were rebuilt to 4-8-0 tank-tender. A total of 30 such engines emerged from this surgical treatment, and after years of SAR operation a number were sold into private ownership.

295

296 One of the last 6th Class 4-6-0s still working was this ex-SAR engine at Koornfontein Colliery, photographed in 1975.

297 It is unusual for locomotives on the collieries to carry names, but this oldtimer, an H-2 of Tavistock Colliery, is very well known.

298 The last 7C 4-8-0 operating in South Africa is at the Hawerklip Mine of Delmas Colliery. The large cab is a characteristic feature of this old SAR engine.

299 In a classic three-quarter 'wedge' shot, TNC's ex-RR Garratt storms up the hill from Bezuidenhoutsrus station with empties for the mine. TNC now uses diesels and its steam is in reserve – a great pity for it had a roster of three Garratts: an 'industrial', the RR 16th Class and an SAR GF, as well as a 12A Mountain, and an old 13th Class 4-8-0 tanker-tender.

300 Near the end of steam at Douglas Colliery: a 12A double-heads with an ex-SAR GM Garratt in 1976. The Garratt was supplied by Dunn's of Witbank, an engineering firm that for many years has acted as a second-hand locomotive agent and provided repair facilities for the many private locomotives operating in the area. Their service has now expanded to include operating and providing maintenance staff at the various railways which use their engines, and their locomotives are frequently transferred from one mine to another to supplement the collieries' own locomotives. But not even these services have been able to stop the diesel invasion of the coalfields.

301 For years the South Witbank Colliery operated an ex-SAR 11th Class 2-8-2, one of two sold to ISCOR during the early 1940s and purchased third-hand by the mine. While the remaining 34 engines were still very much in service on the SAR this one didn't evoke much interest, but now that all the SAR examples have been retired it is well worth looking at. Nine 11s have been sold into private service on various industrial railways, and two additional 11s have arrived at South Witbank to assist in moving coal trucks. They're almost 75 years old now, and still going strong.

302 Landau Colliery paints its locomotives red – and keeps them clean. It has three engines, each a different type: an ex-RR Garratt, a 12A, and the most recent acquisition, this handsome 3BR 4-8-2 purchased from the SAR.

303 Apex Colliery delivers coal to the SAR at Blackhill and operates a three-mile line on which loads move uphill. It has a roster of former SAR engines: two old Class 1 'waterbellies', two 4AR 4-8-2s, and since early 1978, an S Class 0-8-0. Five days a week the mine must deliver 39 wagons for a unit-load to the Highveld Steel Corporation at Clewer, and double-heading is used to move the tonnage, the load being 30 wagons on the grade. On this overcast day in 1976, a clean Class 1 leads an equally clean 4AR.

304 Witbank and Landau Collieries operate a short section of joint track, and the engines of both mines appear in this shot. Purchased new by the collieries, they are 12As to the SAR design with one difference: they have saturated steam boilers. A total of eight were built for four different collieries between 1942 and 1953.

301 303
302 304

232

305 The Hope section of Springbok Colliery has a strange operating arrangement. The mine is located adjacent to the SAR but the washing plant is at the end of a spur two miles away, and so freshly mined coal moves over the line twice. Here a North British tank shunts unwashed coal up the line.

306 Springbok Colliery operates this half-converted North British tank engine. The side tanks have been removed, but the coal bunker and trailing truck remain. It is only the addition of a small four-wheel 'bobber' tender that has made it technically a tender engine.

307 Tweefontein United Colliery is another line which has supplemented its original tank locomotives with SAR power. But before that happened early in 1974, Dusty Durrant photographed this double-header, TUC No. 3 leading No. 1. The engines were originally standard North British 4-8-2 Ts, but were rebuilt to 4-8-0 tender engines, with a large concrete block on the running board which takes the place of the water tank's weight.

306

234

15 North from Pretoria

Pretoria Area

Pretoria is now nearly devoid of main-line steam trains. This is a recent phenomenon, for until the early 1970s it boasted two fully-steam main lines, one busy ore-carrying branch and a lesser branch line. Seven miles north of the city centre, at Wonderboompoort, the double-track main line used to see well over 100 steam trains per day, but this is now electrified and trains not pulled by locomotives feeding off the overhead are nearly all diesel-hauled. Capital Park, the loco shed for Pretoria, which once had an allocation of over 150 engines, now stands at 78, nearly all of which are used for shunting, even 15CAs and some of the once mighty 15Fs.

308

308 SAR's new Blue Train starts its 1 038-mile journey behind steam. This blue S-2 0-8-0 takes the train from the service shed out to the main line where electric locomotives take over for the arrival in Pretoria Station and departure to Johannesburg and westwards.

309 In Pretoria, the nation's capital, main-line steam passenger trains are now only a memory – except for steam excursions which are becoming more and more popular. In 1974, the RSSA organized a train from Johannesburg to Cullinan and back. This immaculate 12A was photographed starting its train on the return journey from Pretoria station, with the city in the background.

309

The Pretoria-Pietersburg Railway

South Africa has never had many trunk-line private railways. The few that were built generally came to grief financially and were taken over by the Government. The Pretoria-Pietersburg Railway was South Africa's second longest private railway (after the New Cape Central), extending 175 miles north to Pietersburg. It was opened to Nylstroom in 1898 and to Pietersburg early in the following year, but it did not survive long under private ownership. As soon as the Anglo-Boer War began in October 1899, the railway's assets were taken over by the Transvaal Government and absorbed into the ZASM.

This railway had an inauspicious beginning for a long-distance main line, as its first three locomotives were tiny 0-6-0 STs used for the construction. However, a larger tank engine arrived in 1897 – a 4-6-0 T originally ordered by the Lourenço Marques, Delagoa Bay and East African Railway (the Portuguese portion of the Eastern Main Line) – and this 35-ton midget had the honour of pulling the first train into Nylstroom ('Nile Stream'). The town was named by the Voortrekkers who had trekked so far north into the interior of Africa that when they came upon a small river running northwards they thought they had reached the Nile, and that Egypt was just over the hill!

A railway couldn't be reliably run with one 'main-line' engine, so six 2-6-4Ts were ordered from Beyer Peacock in 1897. Only five of these very handsome engines arrived, for one fell overboard during a heavy storm in mid-Atlantic. A replacement engine was purchased, and some 4-8-0s, similar to the CGR 7th Class engines, were ordered just before the Government take-over but were never received because of the war.

Today, one would hardly recognise the old P & P. The main line north as far as Pienaars River is double track with a busy suburban service along part of its length, and over 40 trains a day run on the single track beyond. A deviation at Jantingh between Warmbad and Nylstroom which includes a deep cutting and tunnel has eliminated a former banking section, but north of Potgietersrus the line goes over the Ysterberg on the original alignment which includes some long 1 in 50 grades. However, all this is only of academic interest now as the Pretoria-Pietersburg line has been dieselized since 1974. The extension to the Rhodesian border held out longer but succumbed early in 1978.

310 From a koppie between Opblaas and Lunsklip on the climb north from Potgietersrus, there is a superb view of the northbound trains tackling the 1 in 50 grades towards the summit at Lunsklip. In June 1972, an hour's viewing produced a set of double-headed 15CAs followed by a GM, and then this combination of 15CA leading 15F.

311 The Soutpansberg range in the Northern Transvaal runs east to west, forming a barrier between the open grasslands of the Highveld and the bush and tree-covered wilderness to the north. The railway finds its way through the mountains via the spectacular Waterpoort Pass. Since the opening of the through route to Rhodesia in 1975, this line has become busier than ever and until recently a fair number of the trains were steam-powered. Here, a northbound freight powered by a 15F is seen in the narrow confines of the poort.

The Selati Railway and Pietersburg-Tzaneen Service

The Drakensberg Range forms a massive barrier between the inland plateau and the coast in the Cape and Natal before turning northwards through the Transvaal. It comes to an impressive end south of the Soutpansberg, and here is located the northernmost escarpment railway pass in South Africa. It is the Tzaneen-Groenbult section of the Pietersburg to Tzaneen and Kaapmuiden route, originally projected as the Selati Railway back in 1890.

The plan was to build a railway north-west from Komatipoort to the goldfields in the Murchison range, south-east of present-day Tzaneen. The project was riddled with financial misdealings and bribery, and as a Government subsidy was payable on mileage the railway was routed so as to add unnecessary miles. The resulting scandal had international repercussions and only long after things had settled down did the South African Government take up the project, completing it in 1915.

Today the line is effectively two separate railways. A branch to Phalaborwa was opened in 1963, and phosphate and copper traffic moves south to Kaapmuiden, the junction with the Eastern Transvaal Main Line. Before 1971 the southern section of this line ran through the Kruger National Park to the original junction at Komatipoort, but because of heavy traffic – and encounters with elephants – the line was moved to a new junction, 43 miles to the west. At this time steam gave way to diesels which have now been replaced by electric locomotives.

North of Tzaneen heavy fruit traffic moves over the escarpment and down to Pietersburg, eventually reaching the markets of the Witwatersrand and beyond. Mixed steam and diesel working was a feature here for several years, but diesels, released from the lower section early in 1978, have taken over on what was the last impressive mountain-climbing railway in the Transvaal where steam could be seen in action.

313

312 *On the hill*. The entire Tzaneen-Groenbult section is one long mountain pass, but it is the Goudplaas-Groenbult section which climbs over the escarpment. In steam days the daily passenger train from Tzaneen to Pietersburg would arrive at Goudplaas shortly before sunset in winter for the customary service stop before tackling the 1 in 50. In October 1975, 15CA No. 2836 leads 15F No. 2999 three miles above the water stop and 13 miles below the summit.

313 1791 again, before she became famous. This engine was stationed at Pietersburg in 1971 before 15Fs had monopolised workings down to Tzaneen, and in company with 15ARs, 15CAs and 19Ds she performed a variety of services. She is seen working the Tzaneen-Pietersburg passenger, approaching Duiwelskloof.

314 *Men of the Mountains*. Driver Herman Ras and 'passed fireman' Raymond Scott are old hands at running steam up the passes.

315 A unique combination of original and rebuilt 15As. The boiler differences between the two engines are plainly visible in this elevated shot, taken near Baskloof between Goudplaas and Duiwelskloof.

316 Modern branch-line and main-line power combine to move south-bound freight up the short incline facing downhill traffic into Duiwelskloof. The 19D pilot was for many years the standard power on this line; the 15F is representative of the larger power which came later.

317 *Near the end of a day, near the end of an era.* 15CA No. 2836 and 15F No. 2999 stop at the Goudplaas water columns to prepare for the final climb from the Lowveld. Their train is No. 2740, the Pietersburg passenger, and in the hectic next few minutes fires will be cleaned, tenders replenished and moving parts greased. Then the climb will begin. An hour later and 1 400 feet higher, she'll draw into Groenbult, having negotiated a succession of curves, cuts and fills in 16 miles of escarpment-climbing. Ahead: Pietersburg, night, and the end of another run.

Glossary

articulated: term used to describe a steam locomotive whose driving wheels are not grouped on one rigid frame. There are several methods of articulation, among which the Garratt, Mallet, Meyer and Heisler are illustrated in this book

banker, banking engine: an assisting engine attached to the rear of a train to help push it up steep gradients (thus in America: helper)

bogie: a low truck running on two or more pairs of wheels and attached to the fore-part of a locomotive engine or the ends of a long railway carriage by a central pivot, on which it swings freely in passing curves

compensated, uncompensated: friction caused by the interaction of wheel flange and rail on curves causes an additional drag on the locomotive. Today civil engineers compensate for this by reducing the grade on curves. In order to save money this was not done on many lines in early days

donga: South African name for a deep gulley, usually formed by soil erosion

draadkar: Afrikaans railway slang for an electric unit (i.e. electric locomotive)

drag engine: a locomotive designed for slow, heavy goods service

Gammat: the nickname for class GMAM (Afrikaans nickname for a Cape Malay youth)

Granny Smith: the last and usually the most prolific of the season's apple crops

journal box: axle box

kloof: South African name for a valley deeply incised between two mountain ranges or spurs

koppie: a small hillock, often isolated

krantz (krans): cliff or rockface

pick-up: a wayside goods train that clears traffic between its originating and terminating points

pilot: the front engine of a double header

poort: a narrow defile through the mountains

regenerative braking: when electric locomotives work a train downhill the traction motors may be utilised as dynamos to regenerate current for the overhead traction wire (catenary). The magnetic field so produced has a holding-back effect on the armatures of the motors, thus providing a very effective and efficient method of braking the train

road service: running on main or branch lines as distinct from shunting in the yard

staff, tablet: tokens for single-line working without which a driver is not permitted to enter a single track section between two passing stations

tickey: a small South African coin in use before decimalization: three-pence

ton: 2 000 lbs. For ease of calculation, train loads were given in short tons in the SAR employees' Working Time Tables until the metric system was introduced in 1970. With the exception of the ton we have retained imperial measure throughout this book. Engine axleloads are given in long tons of 2 240 lbs

uitlander: Afrikaans term for foreigner

wheel tapper: railway slang for a carriage-and-wagon examiner. A South African institution, he is the reason for the slow and dignified entrance into key stations on long-distance journeys that are so frustrating to train timers.

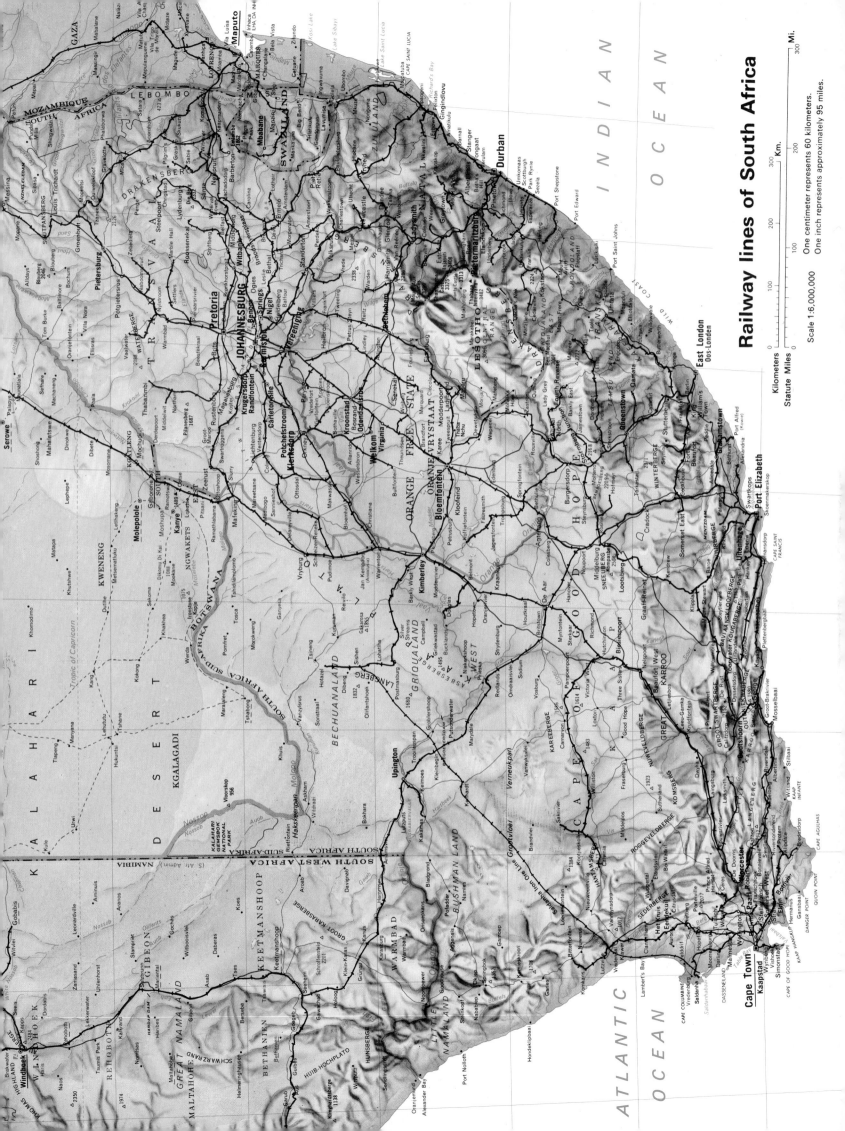

Railway lines of South Africa

Scale 1:6,000,000

One centimeter represents 60 kilometers.
One inch represents approximately 95 miles.

Index

TO STEAM LOCOMOTIVES IN SOUTH AFRICA

Ind.	Industrial
Pre.	Preserved
Reb.	Reboilered
Scr.	Scrapped
Sto.	Stored